D0361952

Vancouver

Chief Editor	Cynthia Clayton Ochterbeck
Editors	Gaven Watkins, Gwen Cannon
Writer	Eric J. Fletcher
Production Coordinator	Natasha George
Cartography	Peter Wrenn
Photo Editors	Lydia Strong, Brigitta L. House
Cover Design	Paris Venise Design
	Paris, 17e

Michelin North America
2540, Boul. Daniel-Johnson, Suite 510
Laval, Québec, H7T 2T9
CANADA
800-361-8236
www.michelin-us.com
email: TheGreenGuide-us@us.michelin.com

Special Sales:

For information regarding bulk sales, customized editions and premium sales, please
contact our Customer Service Departments:

USA – 800-423-0485   **Canada** – 800-361-8236

Michelin Apa Publications Ltd
A joint venture between Michelin and Langenscheidt

No part of this publication may be reproduced in any form
without the prior permission of the publisher.
© 2007 Michelin Apa Publications Ltd

ISBN 2-067-12916-3

Printed and bound in Germany

Note to the reader:

While every effort is made to ensure that all information in this guide is correct and
up-to-date, Michelin Maps and Guides (Michelin North America, Inc.) accepts no liability
for any direct, indirect or consequential losses howsoever caused so far as such can be
excluded by law.

Admission prices listed for sights in this guide are for a single adult, unless otherwise
specified.

Welcome to Vancouver

Table of Contents

Table of Contents

THE MICHELIN STARS

For more than 75 years, travellers have used the Michelin stars to take the guesswork out of planning a trip. Our star-rating system helps you make the best decision on where to go, what to do, and what to see. A three-star rating means it's one of the "absolutelys"; two stars means it's one of the "should sees"; and one star says it's one of the "must sees" – a must if you have the time.

★★★   Absolutely Must See
★★   Really Must See
★   Must See

Three-Star Sights★★★

Butchart Gardens★★★
Pacific Rim National Park Reserve★★★
Royal British Columbia Museum★★★
Stanley Park★★★
UBC Museum of Anthropology★★★
Victoria★★★

Two-Star Sights★

BC Museum of Mining★★
Canada Place★★
Cathedral Grove★★
Chinatown★★
Empress Hotel★★
English Bay Beach★★
Fort Rodd Hill NHS★★
Library Square★★
Lighthouse Park★★
Long Beach★★
O'Keefe Ranch★★
Okanagan Lake★★
Okanagan Valley★★
Radar Hill★★
Robson Street★★
Sea to Sky Highway★★
Stanley Park Seawall★★
Vancouver Aquarium★★
Vancouver Art Gallery★★
Vancouver Maritime Museum★★
Vancouver Museum★★
VanDusen Botanical Garden★★
Whistler★★

One-Star Sights★

BC Place Stadium★
BC Sports Hall of Fame and Museum★
Burnaby Heritage Village★
Capilano Canyon★
Burnaby Village Carousel★
Centre of the Universe★
Christ Church Cathedral★
Craigdarroch Castle★
Cypress Provincial Park★
Desert Interpretive Centre★
Dr. Sun Yat-Sen Classical Chinese Garden★
Fort Langley NHS★
Gastown★
George C. Reifel Bird Sanctuary★
Government Street★
Granville Island★
Granville Island Public Market★
Grouse Mountain★
Gulf of Georgia Cannery NHS★
H. R. MacMillan Space Centre★
Harrison Hot Springs★
Hell's Gate Airtram★
Helmcken House★
Hope★
Hot Springs Cove★
Hotel Vancouver★
Kelowna★
Keremeos Grist Mill★
Lynn Canyon Park★
Marine Building★
Maritime Museum of BC★
Orpheum Theatre★
Pandosy Mission Provincial Heritage Site★
Parliament Buildings★
Queen Elizabeth Park★
Robson Square★
Shannon Falls★
Steveston Village★
Third Beach★
Tofino★
UBC Botanical Garden★
Vancouver Lookout at Harbour Centre Tower★
West Coast Railway Heritage Park★
West End★
Yaletown★

The following abbreviation appears in this list:
NHS National Historic Site.

Listed below are the most popular events in the Vancouver area, including Vancouver Island. Dates (and sometimes names) are subject to change. For the most current information, contact Tourism Vancouver *(604-682-2222; www.tourismvancouver. com)*; Tourism Victoria *(250-953-2033; www.tourism-victoria.com)*; and Tourism BC *(800-435-5622; www.hellobc.com)*.

January

Chinese New Year Festival   604-662-3207
Chinatown   www.vancouverchinesegarden.com

February

Vancouver Storytelling Festival   604-876-2272
Various venues   www.vancouverstorytelling.org

BC Home & Garden Show   604-433-5121
BC Place   www.bchomeandgardenshow.com

Vancouver International Boat Show   604-678-8820
BC Place   www.vancouverboatshow.ca

March

Pacific Rim Whale Festival   250-725-3414
Tofino   www.tourismtofino.com

Vancouver International Dance Festival   604-662-7441
Various venues   www.vidf.ca

April

Vancouver Sun Run 10K   604-689-9441
Downtown Vancouver   www.sunrun.com

World Ski and Snowboard Festival   604-938-3399
Whistler   www.wssf.com

May

New Music West Festival   604-689-2910
Various venues   www.newmusicwest.com

Swiftsure International Yacht Race   250-592-9098
Victoria Inner Harbour   www.swiftsure.org

Vancouver International Children's Festival   604-708-5655
Vanier Park   www.childrensfestival.ca

June

Bard on the Beach Shakespeare Festival   604-739-0559
Vanier Park (through September)
    www.bardonthebeach.com

Dragon Boat Festival   604-688-2382
False Creek   www.adbf.com

Vancouver International Jazz Festival   604-872-5200
Various venues   www.coastaljazz.ca

Vancouver Sun Garden Show   604-687-4780
VanDusen Botanical Garden
    www.vancouvergardenshow.com

July

Canada Day (July 1)
Canada Place & Granville Island
    604-775-8025   www.canadaplace.ca/canadaday
    604-666-5784   www.granvilleisland.com

Theatre Under the Stars   604-687-0174
Stanley Park (through August)   www.tuts.bc.ca

Vancouver Folk Music Festival   604-602-9798
Jericho Beach Park   www.thefestival.bc.ca

**Vancouver International
    Comedy Festival**   604-683-0883
Granville Island   www.comedyfest.com

Vancouver Pride Week   604-687-0955
Various venues   www.vanpride.bc.ca

August

Celebration of Light   604-641-1193
English Bay   www.celebration-of-light.com

Festival Vancouver   604-688-1152
Various venues   www.festivalvancouver.bc.ca

September

Vancouver Fringe Festival   604-257-0350
Various venues   www.vancouverfringe.com

Vancouver International Film Festival   604-683-3456
    www.viff.org

October

**Vancouver International Writers
    & Readers Festival**   604-681-6330
Granville Island   www.writersfest.bc.ca

November

Vancouver Fashion Week   604-338-5849
Stanley Park Pavilion   www.vanfashionweek.com

December

Festival of Lights   604-878-9274
VanDusen Botanical Garden   www.vandusengarden.org

Holiday Festival   604-293-6500
Burnaby Heritage Village   www.city.burnaby.bc.ca

Must Know: Practical Information

WHEN TO GO

The main tourist season for most of Canada, including Vancouver and all of BC, begins the last weekend in May (Victoria Day) and lasts until the first weekend in September (Labour Day). Travel is especially heavy in July and August. Many attractions extend the season to the Thanksgiving weekend (second Monday in October), though tourist crowds diminish considerably after Labour Day.

From early April to mid-May, visitors can usually enjoy comfortable daytime temperatures but expect cool nights in the spring; light showers are likely. July, August and September are ideal for outdoor activities such as sailing, kayaking, canoeing or hiking. Warm, sunny days with temperatures ranging from 22°–25°C/70°–80°F characterize the summer months. Oddly enough, though it is surrounded by water, Vancouver experiences little humid weather in the summer. October can be the best month to visit BC, as the days remain sunny for the most part, and the deciduous trees put on a bright display.

For the sports enthusiast, the BC winter, generally from mid-November to mid-March, offers excellent opportunities to enjoy downhill skiing, cross-country skiing, dogsledding, snowshoeing and snowmobiling. All these activities are available both on Vancouver Island and on the mainland, most notably in Whistler *(see Excursions)*.

Vancouver's Average Seasonal Temperatures

	Jan	Apr	July	Oct
Avg. High	5°C / 41°F	14°C / 57°F	22°C / 72°F	14°C / 57°F
Avg. Low	0°C / 32°F	5°C / 41°F	13°C / 55°F	7°C / 44°F

PLANNING YOUR TRIP

Before you go, contact the following organizations in and around Vancouver for information about sightseeing, accommodations, recreation and annual events.

Tourism Vancouver

200 Burrard St., Vancouver, BC V6C 3L6 Canada
604-683-2000; www.tourismvancouver.com

Tourism BC

865 Hornby St., 8th Floor, Vancouver, BC V6Z 2G3 Canada
250-387-1642 or 800-663-6000; www.hellobc.com

Tourism Victoria

812 Wharf St., Victoria, BC V8W 1T3 Canada
250-953-2033; www.tourismvictoria.com

Tourism Whistler

4010 Whistler Way, Whistler, BC V0N 1B4 Canada
604-932-3928 or 800-944-7853 www.mywhistler.com

Visitor Centres

Tourism Vancouver

200 Burrard St., in Waterfront Centre, Vancouver, BC V6C 3L6 Canada
Open daily 8:30am–6pm.

Vancouver and Victoria Online

In addition to the official tourism Web sites above, try these sites for useful visitor information:
www.canada.com
www.britishcolumbia.com

In the News

The city's leading daily newspaper is the *Vancouver Sun (www.vancouversun.com)*, which provides extensive coverage of arts, entertainment and sports in Vancouver. The *Vancouver Province (www.canada.com/theprovince/)* is a tabloid that offers a more down-to-earth perspective on local affairs.

The *Georgia Straight*, the city's alternative weekly *(www.straight.com)* has the most comprehensive arts and entertainment coverage every Wednesday. *City Food (www. cityfood.com)* is a monthly devoted to restaurant news and reviews, and *Xtra West (www.xtra.ca)*, a free weekly, covers the city's vibrant gay scene.

Tourism Victoria

> 812 Wharf St., Inner Harbour Promenade, Victoria, BC V8W 1T3 Canada
> Open early Sept–May daily 9am–5pm; Jun–early Sept 9am–6:30pm.

Tourism Whistler

> 4230 Gateway Dr., Whistler, BC V0N 1B4 Canada
> Open daily year-round 8am–6pm.

GETTING THERE

By Air – **Vancouver International Airport (YVR)** is located 10km/7mi south of downtown *(604-207-7077; www.yvr.ca)*. The airport services major domestic and international carriers, with nonstop flights from Asia, Europe and North America. Air Canada *(888-247-2262; www.aircanada.com)* and its affiliates provide connections to regions throughout the province.

Taxi service to downtown costs $30. Airport shuttle: Airporter *($13 to downtown; 604-946-8866 or 800-668-3141; www.yvrairporter.com)*. Major car rental agencies are located at the airport.

Airport Fees

Upon departure from some Canadian cities, travellers should be prepared to pay a $5 or higher Airport Improvement Fee before boarding the aircraft. In Vancouver departing passengers pay $15.

By Train – Daily service to **Pacific Central Station** at the east end of downtown *(1150 Station St.)* is provided by **VIA Rail**. Canada's national passenger service, VIA Rail links major cities within the country. In Canada, consult the telephone directory for the nearest office *(from the US, call 800-561-3949; www.viarail.ca)*.

This is also the terminal for Amtrak service from the US *(800-872-7245; www. amtrak.com)*.

By Bus – Pacific Central Station *(1150 Station St.)* is Vancouver's departure point for all buses. For travel from the US or within Canada, contact Greyhound *(604-683-8133; www.greyhound.ca)*.

By Car – Vancouver lies at the westernmost end of the Fraser River Valley in southwestern BC. The main highway access from the east is Highway 1, the Trans-Canada Highway. From the south, access is along Highway 99, which becomes Interstate 5 when it crosses into the US at the Blaine border crossing.

Car Rental Companies

Car Rental Company	Reservations	Internet
Avis	800-331-1212	www.avis.com
Alamo	800-327-9633	www.alamo.com
Budget	800-527-0700	www.budget.com
Dollar	800-800-4000	www.dollar.com
Enterprise	800-325-8007	www.enterprise.com
Hertz	800-654-3131	www.hertz.com
National	800-227-7368	www.nationalcar.com
Thrifty	800-331-4200	www.thrifty.com

GETTING AROUND

The Grid – Most of Vancouver's downtown city streets are laid out in a grid format, with streets running southeast-northwest and northeast-southwest. The main arteries are Granville, Burrard and Denman streets, running northeast to southwest; and Davie and Georgia streets, running southeast to northwest. Georgia Street is the thoroughfare that leads to the Lions Gate Bridge, heading to the North Shore; Granville and Burrard streets cross their namesake bridges over False Creek heading south.

By Foot – Vancouver is best seen on foot. Most downtown sights can be reached within a half-hour (or less) from major hotels; from Stanley Park, at one end of downtown, to Chinatown at the other, is a 30-minute walk. (Do not walk along East Hastings Street, a drug district.) Street numbers rise as you go westward and northward; even numbers are on the east or north sides of the street.

By Car – Vancouver's rush hour is from 7:30am–9am, and 4pm–6pm, but it is mild by North American urban standards. On the other hand, some streets, such as South Granville, are likely to be congested any time between 6am and 10pm. Speed limits, posted in kilometres, are generally 100km/h (60mph) on freeways, 90km/h (55mph) on the Trans-Canada routes, and 80km/h (50mph) on most highways. The speed limit in cities and towns slows to 50km/h (30mph).

Headlights must be turned on at all times. The use of seat belts is mandatory. Parking spaces on downtown streets are limited, and parking regulations are strictly enforced. Limited metered parking is available on non-arterial streets, and parking lots and garages are plentiful. Posted rush-hour restrictions generally prohibit parking and stopping 7am–9am and 4:30pm–6pm *(times vary)*.

Parking – Parking signs are colour-coded: green-and-white signs indicate hours when parking is allowed; red-and-white signs indicate hours when parking is not allowed. Stopping during restricted times could result in your vehicle being towed. Parking spaces identified with a handicapped symbol are reserved for people with disabilities.

Public Transportation – **TransLink** operates an extensive public transportation system of buses, ferries and light rail lines in Vancouver. Hours of operation are: Mon–Sat 6am–1:30am, Sun 9am–1:30am. Adult fares one-way range from $1.50–$3 *(exact fare required; drivers do not sell tickets)*. A Day Pass, good for unlimited one-day travel, is $8. Transfers are free between buses, public ferries and light rail. System maps and timetables are available free of charge. For route information: 604-953-3333 or www.translink.bc.ca.

Taxis – Numerous taxi companies operate in the city under municipal licensing supervision—drivers must demonstrate knowledge of English, be courteous and prove their familiarity with the city. When the "Taxi"sign on the roof of the cab is lit, the vehicle is available for hire. Most downtown runs cost $5–$10 ($1.20–$1.34/km); from downtown to the airport costs $23–$26. Vancouver's major taxi companies include **Yellow Cab** *(604-681-1111)* and **Black Top Cabs** *(604-681-2181)*.

Ferries – *See below.*

GETTING TO VANCOUVER ISLAND AND VICTORIA

Even though Highway 1 starts in Victoria (and goes all the way to Newfoundland), you can't just drive there—the Georgia Strait intervenes. That's why thousands of people hop in their vehicles early on Friday afternoons to get in line for ferry passage to Vancouver Island. The bad news is, there are thousands of those island-hoppers; the good news is, advance planning and flexibility will allow you to bypass the worst of the crush.

By Ferry – **BC Ferries**, the province's ferry service, operates three runs to the island from the Vancouver area *(888-223-3779; www.bcferries.com)*. The Tsawwassen terminal south of the city *(follow Granville St. south to Hwy. 99)* serves ferries crossing to both Swartz Bay (Victoria) and Duke Point (Nanaimo and the rest of the island). The Horseshoe Bay terminal in West Vancouver *(at the continental end of Hwy. 1, take Georgia St. west across the Lions Gate Bridge)* serves ferries to Nanaimo, as well as other destinations. All three runs to the island consist of large boats departing roughly every two hours. Once you reach the island, it's about a half-hour into downtown Victoria from Swartz Bay; and three hours from Nanaimo to Tofino. Passage for a vehicle and driver varies by season and day, but peaks at about $35. To beat the crowds, make an advance reservation. The ferries' reserved boarding service carries a premium—$15 one way—but it's worth it.

By Air – Several airline operations fly between Vancouver and the island. The two most popular lines both depart from downtown sites near Canada Place.

Helijet *(800-665-4354; www.helijet.com)* flies Bell Jet Ranger craft to a landing pad at the entrance to Victoria's Inner Harbour. Passage takes about 25 minutes, and the view of the strait and Gulf Islands is wonderful.

Harbour Air *(depart from downtown floatplane base just west of Canada Place; 800-665-0212; www.harbour-air.com)* flies floatplanes—mostly the DeHavilland Beavers and Otters that are considered some of the sturdiest planes ever built. Passage to Victoria takes about 40 minutes.

AREA CODES

In greater Vancouver you must dial the area code plus the seven-digit number to make a local phone call. Before you leave, check with your home carrier to make sure your cell phone will operate in Canada.

Vancouver and the Lower Mainland, including Whistler: **604** and **778**
Rest of British Columbia, including Victoria and Vancouver Island: **250**

TIPS FOR SPECIAL VISITORS

Disabled Travellers – Most public buildings, public transit and ferries, and many attractions, restaurants and hotels in Vancouver provide wheelchair access. Disabled parking is provided and the law is strictly enforced. For details, contact Tourism Vancouver. Many national and provincial parks have restrooms and other facilities for the disabled (such as wheelchair-accessible nature trails or tour buses). For details about a specific park, call 888-773-8888 or check online at www.pc.gc.ca. Passengers who will need special assistance with train travel should contact **VIA Rail Special Needs Services** *(888-842-7245 or 800-268-9503/TDD; www.viarail.ca)*. For information about bus travel, contact **Greyhound Canada** *(800-661-8747 or 800-345-3109/TDD; www.greyhound.ca)*.

Local Lowdown – Additional information is available from the **BC Office for Disability Issues** *(250-387-3813 or 250-387-3555/TDD)*; or from the *We're Accessible Quarterly (to request a copy, call 604-576-5075)*.

Senior Citizens – Many attractions, hotels, restaurants, entertainment venues and public transportation systems offer discounts to visitors age 62 or older (proof of age may be required). Canada's national parks usually offer discount fees for seniors. For more information, contact the **Canadian Association for the 50 Plus** *(CARP; 800-363-9736; www.50plus.com)*. Visiting seniors should feel free to ask specific businesses if a discount is available.

INTERNATIONAL VISITORS

In addition to local tourism offices, visitors may obtain information from the nearest Canadian embassy or consulate in their country of residence. Embassies of other countries are located in Canada's capital, Ottawa. Many foreign countries also maintain consulates in Vancouver. For further information on all Canadian embassies and consulates abroad, contact the Web site of the Canadian Department of Foreign Affairs and International Trade: *www.dfait-maeci.gc.ca*.

Entry Requirements – As of January 2007, citizens of the US need a valid passport or Air NEXUS card to visit Canada and return by air. A driver's license and a birth certificate together are currently accepted to enter Canada and return to the US by land or sea; parents bringing children into Canada are strongly advised to carry birth certificates. As of 2008, only a passport or secure passport card will be accepted to return to the US. All other visitors to Canada must have a valid passport and, in some cases, a visa *(see list of countries at www.cic.gc.ca/english/visit/visas.html)*. No vaccinations are necessary. Check with the Canadian embassy or consulate in your home country about entry regulations and proper travel documents.

Canada Customs – Visitors over 18 entering Canada may bring 1.14 litres of liquor or 1.5 litres of wine or 24 cans of beer without paying duty or taxes. Tobacco is limited to 200 cigarettes or 200 grams/7oz of loose product. Gifts totalling $60 Canadian may be brought in duty-free. All prescription drugs should be clearly labeled and for personal use only; it's best to carry a copy of the prescription. For details, call the Border Information Service *(800-467-9999, Vancouver)* or write to Border Services Agency, Ottawa, Ontario, K1A 0L5 Canada *(www.cbsa-asfc.gc.ca)*. Canada has stringent legislation on firearms—do not bring any weapons to the border. For further information on entry of fire-arms, contact the Canadian Centre for Firearms *(284 Wellington St., Ottawa, Ontario K1A 0H8 Canada; 800-731-4000; www.cfc-ccaf.gc.ca)*. Parents bringing children into Canada are strongly advised to bring along birth certificates, especially if just one parent is travelling with children.

Crossing the Border – The US-Canada border crossing at Blaine is the busiest west of Michigan. Lines can grow long on weekends and holidays; the best time to cross, either way, is early morning weekdays and Sundays. It is much easier heading north into Canada, which has 10 lanes for border inspection, than returning to the States, which has just three lanes.

When crossing the border, do not try to carry contraband. Don't take any weapons into Canada, or Cuban cigars into the States. Passports are by far the best identification; birth certificates will do, but you can no longer pass, either direction, with just a driver's license or a voter registration card.

Money and Currency Exchange – Visitors can exchange currency at downtown banks as well as at Vancouver International Airport. Banks, stores, restaurants and hotels accept travellers' cheques with photo identification. To report a lost or stolen credit card: American Express *(800-528-4800)*; Diners Club *(800-234-6377)*; MasterCard *(800-307-7309)*; or Visa *(800-336-8472)*.

All prices shown in this guide are in Canadian dollars unless otherwise specified.

Driving in Canada – Drivers from the US may use valid state-issued licenses. Visitors from elsewhere should obtain an International Driving Permit through their national automobile association in order to rent a car. Drivers must carry vehicle registration and/or rental contract, and proof of automobile insurance at all times. Gasoline is sold by the litre. Vehicles in Canada are driven on the right-hand side of the road.

Electricity – Voltage in Canada is 120 volts AC, 60 Hz. Foreign-made appliances may need AC adapters (available at specialty travel and electronics stores) and North American two-prong, flat-blade plugs.

Taxes and Tipping – Prices displayed in Canada do not include sales tax *(see sidebar above)*. It is customary to give a small gift of money—a **tip**—for services rendered, to waiters *(15–20% of bill)*, porters *($1 per bag)*, chamber maids *($1 per day)* and taxi drivers *(15% of fare)*.

Vancouver Taxes

In Vancouver (as in the rest of Canada) the Goods and Services Tax (GST) is a 6% tariff that is added to most goods and services. British Columbia also charges a 7% provincial sales tax (PST). There is a 10% lodging tax in Vancouver.

Time Zone – Vancouver is located in the Pacific Standard Time zone (PST), eight hours behind Greenwich Mean Time and three hours behind New York City.

Measurement Equivalents

Metric System – Canada has partially adopted the International System of weights and measures. Weather temperatures are given in Celsius (°C), milk and wine are sold by millilitres and litres, and grocery items are measured in grams. All distances and speed limits are posted in kilometres (to obtain the approximate equivalent in miles, multiply by 0.6). Some examples of metric conversions are:

        1 ounce = 28 grams (gm)
        1 pound = 0.45 kilograms (kg)
        1 inch   = 2.54 centimetres (cm)
        1 foot   = 30.48 centimetres
        1 mile   = 1.6 kilometres (km)
        1 quart = 0.94 litres
        1 gallon = 3.78 litres

Temperature Equivalents

Degrees Fahrenheit	95°	86°	77°	68°	59°	50°	41°	32°	23°	14°
Degrees Celsius	35°	30°	25°	20°	15°	10°	5°	0°	-5°	-10°

Important Numbers	
Emergency (Police, Ambulance, Fire Department, 24hrs)	**911**
Police (non-emergency)	604-717-3535
Crime Stoppers	800-222-8477
24-hour Medical and Dental Clinic	604-877-0664
24-hour Pharmacy:	
Shoppers Drug Mart, 1125 Davie St.	604-669-2424
Weather	604-664-9010
Road Conditions	604-660-9770
Canadian Automobile Association	604-293-2222

ACCOMMODATIONS

For a list of specific suggested accommodations, see Must Stay.

Reservations Services:

Tourism Vancouver – 604-683-2000; www.tourismvancouver.com.

Tourism BC – 250-387-1642 or 800-663-6000; www.hellobc.com.

Western Canada Bed & Breakfast Innkeepers Association – www.wcbbia.com.

Major hotel and motel chains with locations in Vancouver

Property	Phone	Web site
Best Western	800-780-7234	www.bestwestern.com
Choice Hotels	877-424-6423	www.choicehotels.com
Days Inn	800-329-6423	www.daysinn.com
Delta Hotels	877-814-7706	www.deltahotels.com
Fairmont	800-441-1414	www.fairmont.com
Four Seasons	800-332-3442	www.fourseasons.com
Hilton	800-221-2424	www.hilton.com
Holiday Inn	800-465-4329	www.holidayinn.com
Marriott	888-236-2427	www.marriott.com
Radisson Inn	888-201-1718	www.radisson.com
Ramada Inn	800-272-6232	www.ramada.com
Sheraton	800-325-3535	www.sheraton.com
Westin	800-937-8461	www.westin.com

Campgrounds – BC Parks: 800-689-9025; www.elp.gov.bc.ca/bcparks.

Hostels – There are three fine, large hostels in Vancouver, two downtown and one in Kitsilano *(see Must Stay)*. Many other destinations in BC have hostels; contact Hostelling International-Canada *(800-663-5777 or www.hihostels.ca)* for other hostels in the province.

SPORTS

Vancouver is a great place to be a spectator at sporting events. The city's major professional sports teams include:

Sport/Team	Season	Venue	Info#	Web site
Football/BC Lions (Canadian Football League)	mid-Jun–Nov	BC Place	604-589-7627	www.bclions.com
Hockey/ Vancouver Canucks (National Hockey League)	Oct–Apr	GM Place	604-899-4625	www.canucks.com
Baseball/ Vancouver Canadians (Northwest League of Professional Baseball)	Apr–Sept	Nat Bailey Stadium	604-872-5232	www.canadiansbaseball.com

Vancouver

Pacific Rim Paradise: Vancouver, British Columbia

Sparkling Vancouver is truly a city of the world. Poised at North America's Pacific Rim—and at the forefront of urban life—this cosmopolitan city boasts a spectacular natural setting, a thriving economy, high marks from both residents and visitors, and a level of cultural diversity matched by few other metropolitan areas.

It's all about lifestyle here. Vancouver sure seems to have it all: a mild climate, fabulous restaurants, world-class hotels, great cultural attractions, recreational opportunities galore. Add in a healthy economy and it's no wonder that Vancouver has been rated the "most liveable city in the world."

The place now called Vancouver was once just big trees surrounded by shellfish-laden beaches and salmon-rich waters, and populated by the First Nations peoples. Although the waters of British Columbia were first explored by Spanish seafarers, it was Captain George Vancouver who charted the area for Britain in 1793. The first European settlers, trappers and traders, established posts for the Hudson's Bay Company in the early 1800s. In 1858 the discovery of gold in the BC interior brought global attention to the region—but the real wealth of the coast turned out to be timber.

Fast Facts

History: First European settlement was established in 1863; Vancouver was incorporated in 1886.
Population: 585,000 (city); 2,000,000 (18 Lower Mainland municipalities)
Distance to the US Border: 24 miles
Annual precipitation: 46 inches
Top 10 languages: English, Mandarin, Cantonese, Punjabi, German, Italian, French, Tagalog (Filipino), Spanish, Russian
Mother Tongue: Half of Vancouver's school-age children were raised speaking a language other than English.

In 1863 the first sawmill was built on Burrard Inlet, and as the towering old-growth Douglas firs and western red cedars were felled, development sprang up in the clearings. European, Asian and American immigrants flocked to BC in the latter half of the 19C to work in the timber or fishing industries, and when Canadian Pacific Railway chose Burrard Inlet as the terminus for its transcontinental rail line in 1885, Vancouver's future was assured.

Pacific Rim Paradise: Vancouver, British Columbia

Today Vancouver thrives as Canada's Pacific hub, the largest port in the country—trade in BC as a whole supports 1 in 4 jobs. Tourism has assumed huge significance, with 9 million visitors a year to Vancouver. And the film industry spends more than $1 billion annually in and around the city.

Filmmakers like the fact that BC's diverse landscape means that somewhere within a few hours of Vancouver is a setting that can substitute for almost any place in the world, and the city's famously temperate climate assures virtually nonstop production. That climate also enables BC growers to produce a vast array of fruits, vegetables, herbs and wines that Vancouver chefs use, blending continental and Asian influences with Pacific seafood, to create a distinctive regional fare known as West Coast cuisine.

For the visitor, Vancouver is a remarkably user-friendly city. Although there are no freeways, travel from the airport to downtown takes less than a half-hour. Once you're downtown, the vast majority of attractions are within walking distance— Stanley Park, the Art Gallery, Canada Place, Gastown, Chinatown, Yaletown. Canadians are uniformly helpful and friendly, and the currency exchange rate has traditionally favoured those spending American dollars, British pounds and euros. On top of all that, everywhere you look is spectacular scenery: glistening blue water, majestic forests, and towering snowcapped mountains. How could you ask for more?

Sea-to-Sky Games: Winter Olympics 2010

The Vancouver-Whistler bid for the 2010 Winter Olympics was accepted by the International Olympic Committee in July 2003. The 2010 games will be the first Olympics in Canada since the 1988 Calgary winter games. Here's the lowdown:

- **When**: February 12–28, 2010
- **Spectators expected**: 250,000; global TV audience – 2 billion
- **Participants**: 5,000 team members from 50 countries
- **Events in Vancouver**: hockey, curling, skating
- **Events in West Vancouver**: snowboarding, freestyle skiing
- **Events in Whistler**: Alpine and Nordic skiing, bobsled, luge

Green space is everywhere in Vancouver and its surrounding suburbs—little half-block play areas, undeveloped outlying parcels of wetland or woods. It's the big city parks that get the most attention, though. Recreational areas like Stanley Park and the provincial parks on the North Shore offer gardens and places to play galore, along with a vast array of attractions ranging from gourmet restaurants to beaches.

Stanley Park★★★

At the northwest end of downtown, access via Georgia & Davie Sts. 604-257-8400. www.city.vancouver.bc.ca/parks. Open 24hrs daily.

Stanley Park is the unquestioned highlight of Vancouver, one of North America's best city parks. Urban residents are not only justifiably proud of their famous park, they use it avidly—and visitors are just as fond of the park's attractions. It's big (405ha/1,000 acres), beautiful, accessible and uncrowded. A visit to Stanley Park can be as simple as a 20-minute stroll along the seawall path. Or it can be as elaborate as an interactive sea-mammal experience at the **Vancouver Aquarium★★** *(see Musts for Kids),* followed by a walk through deep forests to an elegant dinner at a restaurant overlooking the Strait of Georgia. Stanley Park has wildlife, woods, sandy beaches, children's play areas, statues and totems, gardens and pools. Film crews use the park as a stand-in for woods worldwide.

You can accomplish a quick driving tour *(see p 24)* of the park in a morning, following the counterclockwise drive that skirts its perimeter and touches on most of the high points. However, not to set off on foot is a mistake, since much of the park's finest territory lies beyond the roadway.

It's commonly assumed that Stanley Park's acres of Western red cedar, Douglas fir and western hemlock are old-growth forest. They're not; most of the park

---

A Park for the People?

In the late 19C Vancouver's first city council asked the federal government to preserve the land for Stanley Park and deed it to the city; it had been a military reserve, but it was not untouched forest. The transfer took place in 1888, and the park was dedicated the following year by its namesake, Lord Peter Stanley, Canada's governor-general. Though the city's founders showed amazing foresight to preserve such a magnificent piece of land, their motives were not wholly altruistic: The park was meant to boost the viability of housing developments in the West End.

was logged before 1870 ("high-graded"—only the biggest and best timber was removed). The nearest true old-growth forest is across Burrard Inlet at **Lighthouse Park★★**. However, logging ceased so long ago in Stanley Park that much of its forest is now approaching maturity, and as you hike and bike along some of the interior trails, you'll see some impressively large trees—despite the loss of thousands of trees in a violent wind storm in December 2006.

Visiting Stanley Park

It's best to arrive by bus or on foot, as parking poses a problem—even if you can find a space, it costs up to $2 per hour (the pay machines must be fed; the parking police are vigilant). The most popular attractions (Vancouver Aquarium, the Totem Park, Prospect Point, Third Beach and Second Beach) are also the most crowded. If you can, arrive early, find a parking place along Stanley Park Drive, the circumferential road, and plan to walk to the sights. A stroll from Third Beach to the Aquarium, for example, takes just 15 to 20 minutes.

Other tips:

- Stop first at the visitor centre, which is located about .8km/ .5mi in on Stanley Park Drive near the aquarium entrance, and grab a map.
- Do *not* feed the cute squirrels, raccoons and other critters— they are wild and they do bite.
- If you want to swim, Second Beach is best in the morning; Third Beach is best in the afternoon.
- Use the free park shuttle bus: 15 stops at popular destinations (10am–6:30pm).

Lost Lagoon Nature House

South side of Lost Lagoon, at northwest end of Robson St. 604-257-8544. www.stanleyparkecology.ca. Open Jul–Sept Tue–Sun 10am–7pm, Sept–Feb weekends 9:30am–4pm, Mar–Jun Fri noon–4pm & weekends 9:30am–4:30pm. This compact facility is an interpretive centre for Stanley Park, operated by a local ecology organization. Periodic programs cover everything from the creatures that live in the lagoon to the life cycle of the old-growth forest that Stanley Park is becoming again. Volunteers are on-site to answer questions about the park and distribute information.

Scenic Drive★

The 10km/6mi drive that circles the park perimeter will take you past all its significant sights. Traffic moves counterclockwise, starting at the park entrance at the end of West Georgia Street. Stanley Park Drive first swings around Coal Harbour, passing the Vancouver Rowing Club and Royal Vancouver Yacht Club. Between the two, to the north, is the entrance to the Vancouver Aquarium, and the main park information kiosk. A quarter-mile farther on is the park's famed collection of **totem poles★** *(see sidebar),* occupying a site where a Coast Salish village stood 150 years ago.

Nine o'clock gun – At Hallelujah Point, just past the totems, this gun is fired every evening—since 1894—to mark a historic fishing curfew. Brockton Point holds a replica of the prow of the **Empress of Japan,** one of the first clipper ships to call at the port of Vancouver. Just past that, the **Girl in a Wet Suit** statue, placed on a rock in 1984, mimics the legendary mermaid sculpture that graces Copenhagen's harbour.

Prospect Point★ – The road climbs to a bluff at Prospect Point, offering wide **views★** of the North Shore with snowcapped mountains behind, and across the Strait of Georgia to Vancouver Island. A half-mile farther on, stop at the **Hollow Tree,** a much-photographed cedar stump, to see how many people you can fit inside.

Third Beach★ – This broad expanse of golden sand is perfect for picnicking and admiring the views. **Ferguson Point** offers more views from a bluff; and the Stanley Park Pool at **Second Beach★** is packed with bathers on warm days *(see Musts for Outdoor Fun).* The road winds by the park's excellent pitch-and-putt golf course, bypassing Lost Lagoon (a slightly brackish pond) to return to Georgia Street.

Totem Poles★

Carved from cedar logs, totems are traditional Native monuments that depict the animals and spirits central to the First Nations' pantheistic belief systems. Ravens, bears, salmon, eagles, frogs, whales and wolves are common figures. An interpretive centre near the totems explains traditional Native village life, and a shop offers guidebooks and posters. Artists represented include Bill Reid *(see Museums)* and Chief Mungo Martin, two legendary Native carvers.

Stanley Park Seawall★★

Ready for a walk? This marvelous 9.5km/6mi bike and pedestrian path was the lifework of stonemason James Cunningham (1878–1963). A 9.5km/5.9mi barrier of 46kg/101-pound granite blocks built over the course of 46 years to withstand the battering of winter storms, the seawall follows much the same route as the driving tour described here, but affords better views. At Prospect Point, watch for **Siwash Rock★**, a small sea stack that, according to Native legend, represents the petrified soul of a virtuous member of the Salish tribe.

Gardens – Flower fans will want to visit the lovely formal **rose gardens** *(along Pipeline Rd.)*, which reach their peak in June, and the **rhododendron gardens** *(south of Lost Lagoon)*, where hundreds of different varieties burst into bloom in May and June.

Trails – More than a dozen well-maintained trails crisscross the interior of the park, offering hikers and bikers the opportunity to find solitude in the woods. **Lake Trail** and **Tatlow Walk** are two of the best; you can access them from Stanley Park Drive near Second Beach.

Vancouver Aquarium★★, **Children's Farmyard** and **Miniature Train** – *See Musts for Kids.*

Big Cedar

In the 1950s the National Geographic Society declared a Western red cedar on the park's western slope the world's largest. Found along the uphill path from Third Beach to the Hollow Tree, the cedar does not seem all that remarkable as you approach—until you stand at its base and circle the 3.6m/12ft-diameter trunk. The tree died in the 1990s, possibly as a result of topping that was done years before.

Near the Third Beach concession, a red alder with four trunks is reckoned to be the largest alder in Canada; and a bigleaf maple in the woods southeast of the Hollow Tree is considered the largest such maple in the country. That's a lot of big-tree-dom in one small area—but imagine what trees might have been here before the park was logged!

The Hollow Tree itself, right along Stanley Park Drive a half-mile south of Prospect Point, was once sufficiently big enough that today its shell-like stump is a popular photo op, with groups of people standing inside. Springboard notches on the side mark the place where sawyers stood in the 1870s to bring down this huge cedar.

VanDusen Botanical Garden★★

5251 Oak St. at 37th Ave. 604-878-9274. www.vandusen.org. Open year-round daily 10am to dusk. Closed Dec 25. $8.25.

Imagine houses filling this lovely spot, instead of the colourful botanical garden. That's what it came perilously close to being. Once the site of a golf club for the nearby **Shaughnessy** mansion district *(see Neighbourhoods),* the land that now holds VanDusen garden was slated to be turned into a residential housing development in the 1970s. Citizen activism spurred the city to buy the 55-acre piece of rolling ground, and it has since grown into a horticultural showpiece.

The garden's overall purpose is to demonstrate the horticultural possibilities offered by Vancouver's mild climate—a notion illustrated by the healthy copse of palms growing beneath mature Douglas firs and cedars by the entrance. Inside the garden, plantings range from hollies to bamboos, magnolias to birches.

Numerous theme gardens scattered about the site include a Japanese meditation garden, an herb garden, a perennial garden, a maze and a fern dell. The wide variety (7,500 different plants) ensures that something is in bloom almost year-round. The gift shop and bookstore focus on material promoting horticulture in the Lower Mainland.

Winter Garden – This collection of fragrant witch hazels, winter hazels and winter-blooming jasmine, as well as hellebores and other exotic off-season bloomers, is enchanting in January and February, belying winter's gray skies.

Canadian Heritage Garden – Native Canadian plants here focus on those that clothed, housed and fed First Nations people and pioneers, ranging from red cedar to Saskatoon berries. Plants from both east and west, and the prairie in between, are included.

The Palm Gardens

Vancouver's much-acclaimed "mild" climate is given exquisite testimony in several gardens near English Bay Beach, at the intersection of Denman and Davie streets. Here city horticulturists have planted several dozen palm trees and other tropical plants (including hardy bananas!) that thrive in the protected, south-facing location. Though frosts do occur in the area, the waters of English Bay moderate the cold, and the West End high rises block the chilliest northerly winds. On a sunny summer day, with palm fronds waving in the breeze, you could almost believe you were in the Caribbean.

Queen Elizabeth Park★

33rd Ave. & Cambie St. 604-257-8400.
www.city.vancouver.bc.ca/parks. Open
24hrs daily.

The highest point in Vancouver, a 154m/505ft hillock, is the pinnacle of this 52.5ha/130-acre park, which spreads across the largely open hillside. Six million visitors a year make Queen Elizabeth the city's second most popular park. The northwest end of the park is an arboretum that holds almost all the trees native to Canada, as well as many specimens from Europe and elsewhere in North America. **Nat Bailey Stadium,** on the park's southern end, is the summer home of the Vancouver Canadians, the city's minor-league baseball team *(see Practical Information).*

Bloedel Floral Conservatory

At the park's high ground sits Bloedel Conservatory, a geodesic-style greenhouse that houses 500 tropical plants and 150 birds. Paths wander amid the gardens and aviaries. A plexiglass dome covers the second-largest domed greenhouse in the world.

Quarry Gardens

Occupying a former stone quarry, this multi-level garden with its colourful annuals and wide sweeping lawns brings to mind Victoria's Butchart Gardens, though it's not quite as formal *(see Excursions).*

Viewpoint

Climb to the city's highest point (154m/505ft) here for a wonderful **panorama★★** of Vancouver to the north, and the North Shore Mountains beyond—including the twin "Lions" peaks for which Lions Gate is named. To the east, you can see the snowy cone of Mount Baker. To the west, the Georgia Strait and the mountains of Vancouver Island loom in the distance.

Seasons Restaurant

In Queen Elizabeth Park at 33rd Ave. &
Cambie St. 604-874-8008.
www.sequoiarestaurants.com.

Seasons boasts views almost as broad as those from the park's pinnacle. Bill Clinton and Boris Yeltsin had dinner here during their summit in 1993; today, brunch is the most popular meal, with dishes ranging from carrot and ginger soup to poached black cod.

Dr. Sun Yat-Sen Classical Chinese Garden★

578 Carrall St., Chinatown. 604-662-3207. www.vancouverchinesegarden.com. Open May–mid-Jun 10:30am–6pm; mid-Jun–Aug 9:30am–7pm; Sept 10am–6pm; Oct–Apr 10am–4:30pm. $8.75.

You're bound to find serenity amid the intricately laid patios, elaborately decorated pavilions and carefully positioned rocks of the Sun Yat-Sen garden. The stucco, tile-roofed walls of the compound shelter one of the finest formal gardens in North America. Indeed, this was the first true Ming Dynasty-style garden built in North America. In 1886 Chinese artisans crossed the Pacific to help create it, bringing with them classical stone, tile, brick and timber.

Like all Chinese gardens, this one focuses as much on the man-made framework for growing things, as on the plants themselves. Each plant is chosen for its symbolic meaning, and the garden celebrates all four seasons with azaleas and trees such as maples, magnolias and evergreens. Moon gates and open portals offer artful views into courtyards and meditation nooks. Frequent guided tours *(included in price of admission)* explain the painstaking construction and significance of every element, none of which are random.

The Tao of Gardening

Japanese and classical Chinese gardens have many elements in common—rocks, ponds, carefully placed plants, man-made artifacts such as bridges, courtyards and shelters. How do you tell the difference between the two? Japanese gardens use natural features to create meditative spaces, whereas Chinese gardens use artfully designed meditative spaces to represent nature. The Sun Yat-Sen garden was built by Chinese artisans using traditional tools, materials, plants and techniques, blending the four traditional elements: rocks, water, plants and buildings. Limestone rocks represent mountains, and the three key plants are bamboo, representing resilience; pines, representing strength; and plums, whose blossoms symbolize rebirth. The Taoist yin-yang balance is represented by rocks and buildings (yang, or hard), and water, which is the soft, or yin, element.

UBC Botanical Garden★

6804 S.W. Marine Dr., on the University of British Columbia campus. 604-822-9666. www. ubcbotanicalgarden.org. Open mid-Mar–mid-Oct daily 10am–6pm. Rest of the year daily 10am–5pm. $6 (late Oct–early Mar by donation).

The largest rhododendron collection in Canada—400 varieties—nestles beneath the native hemlock trees in this 28ha/70-acre garden that melds Northwest species with horticultural plants. Theme gardens are scattered throughout the property. The setting, on a bluff overlooking the Strait of Georgia, adds to the pleasure of a visit.

In case the gardening bug bites you during your visit, you can buy seeds from some of the plants that grow in the botanical garden at the site's gift shop, along with a nice selection of gardening books, tools and accessories.

Alpine Garden – Specimens from mountains around the world—from Borneo to Russia—are included in one of the largest alpine collections in North America.

Asian Garden – Magnolias (one of the largest collections on earth), rhododendrons and azaleas predominate in this sprawling garden in the shade of mature conifers.

Food Garden – Bearing everything from kiwis to kohlrabi, the raised beds and fruit borders of this garden illustrate what can be grown in household gardens.

Native Garden – You'll find hundreds of species native to BC in this plot.

Physic Garden – Both old and new medicinal plants are here, from yarrow and rose hips to periwinkle, source of a modern drug used to treat leukemia.

A Rhododendron By Any Other Name

Would you be surprised to know that those rhododendrons growing in your yard are related to blueberries? Well, they are. They're also related to azaleas, heather and mountain laurel—all members of the heath family, Ericaceae. More than a thousand species have been identified within the genus *Rhododendron*. Known for their shiny dark green leaves and large bright pink, purple or white flowers, rhododendrons grow all over the world, from the Arctic to the tropics.

Nitobe Memorial Garden

S.W. Marine Dr., on the University of British Columbia campus. Enter at Gate 4. 604-878-9274. www.nitobe.org. Open mid-Mar–mid-Oct daily 10am–6pm. Rest of the year non-holiday weekdays 10am–2:30pm. $4 (late Oct–early Mar by donation).

Inside the walls of this 1ha/2.5-acre enclave you'll find a carefully constructed Japanese garden that focuses on traditional elements of balance and serenity. Paths wander amid ponds, meditation gardens, azaleas, flowering cherries and irises. In the fall, the Asian maples bear brilliant crimson and orange leaves. Bridges, benches and carefully placed stones complete the meditative atmosphere. The garden honours **Dr. Inazo Nitobe** (1862–1933), a diplomat and longtime BC resident devoted to bridging the gap between Japanese and North American cultures.

With its authentic teahouse, the **Tea Garden** inside Nitobe is considered to be one of the most authentic outside Japan. "I am in Japan," proclaimed that country's current emperor when he toured the garden in the 1990s.

Pacific Spirit Regional Park

Between 4th Ave. & Marine Dr. in the Point Grey section of Vancouver, also south to Fraser River. Information centre at 4915 W. 16th Ave. 604-224-5739. www.gvrd.bc.ca/parks.

This sprawling expanse of woods borders Southwest Marine Drive on its approach to the University of British Columbia campus. Its extensive network of hiking trails *(20km/33mi)* and biking trails *(14km/23mi)* includes many paths that lead downhill to the shore of English Bay, offering seclusion and light-dappled forest. Along the way, Pacific Spirit meets Jericho Beach Park (a shoreline greenbelt that offers sandy beaches and picnic areas) and farther west toward UBC, Wreck Beach, a legendary expanse of sand where clothing is optional. On the more northerly stretches of bluff-bordered pebble shore, you'll have spectacular **views**★★ of the North Shore Mountains.

With sections spreading south completely across the Point Grey Peninsula, the entire park at 763ha/1,885 acres ranks as the largest green space in Vancouver—nearly twice as large as Stanley Park. Almost entirely logged in the 19C, it has since sprung up again into a lush, largely deciduous forest in which a dozen kinds of ferns grow in the filtered light. The southeast end of the park includes **Camosun Bog,** a rare example of a once-common peat marshland. A boardwalk allows you to experience the bog without damaging it.

North Shore Parks

Here's a list of must-visit parks in North and West Vancouver. *For detailed descriptions of individual sites, see Nearby Vancouver.*

Lighthouse Park★★

Marine Dr., 8km/5mi northwest of downtown via Lions Gate Bridge; follow Marine Dr. west to Beacon Lane.

This 79ha/105 acre park harbours one of the area's last major parcels of untouched old-growth forest. Its vantage point on a Howe Sound headland means you'll get stunning **views**★★★ of Vancouver across the water.

Cypress Provincial Park★

12km/7mi northwest of downtown via Lions Gate Bridge & Hwy. 1 west to Cypress Mountain Rd.

Ski areas, fir and hemlock forests and breathtaking **views**★★★ are highlights of the 3,000ha/7,400-acre recreational area.

Lynn Canyon Park★

17km/10.5mi north of Vancouver via Lions Gate Bridge to Hwy. 1. Take the Lynn Valley Rd. exit, turn right on Lynn Valley Rd. and right on Peters Rd. to the park.

This North Shore gorge boasts a 33m/109ft-long **suspension bridge**★ and a spectacular waterfall.

Ambleside Park

6km/4mi north of Vancouver via Lions Gate Bridge and west on Marine Dr.

Locals favour this strip of green space interspersed with sandy beaches that starts at the Capilano River and hugs the shoreline for several miles west.

Capilano River Regional Park

9km/6mi north of Vancouver via Lions Gate Bridge to Hwy. 1 to Capilano Rd. Take the exit for Grouse Mountain and continue north to the park.

Hiking trails within the 142ha/350-acre regional park cross the river and climb into deep forest.

Take some time to get to know Vancouver's distinctive neighbourhoods. One of the densest residential districts in North America, the West End also forms the heart of the city's vibrant gay and lesbian community. Kitsilano, a slightly gentrified former hippie haven, is now a wonderful place for families to live and work. Dazzling and energetic, hip Yaletown borders a massive urban development, Concord Place, which has transfigured what was left of the Expo '86 grounds. Chinatown is one of the best areas for a morning stroll in any city.

Chinatown★★

Bounded by Keefer, Abbott & Hastings Sts. & Gore Ave.
www.virtualvancouver.com/chinatown.html.

Though Vancouver's Chinatown is small by North American neighbourhood standards, it is big by Chinatown standards—the third-largest, exceeded only by Chinatowns in New York and San Francisco. It dates back almost 150 years, to the days when Chinese laborers were brought across the Pacific to build the Canadian railroads and wagon roads; its continuing vitality reflects the mid-1990s exodus from Hong Kong to Canada, as well as Canada's policy of welcoming immigrants. To this day, more than half the district's residents list Mandarin or Cantonese as their native language.

It's best to explore Chinatown on foot, so you can take in the sights, sounds, smells and tastes of the dynamic Asian cultural mix; start at Pender and Carrall streets, head east three blocks to Gore, then south a block and back west on Keefer Street. Along the way, the exotic world of Asian life flavours every step. Seafood stalls offer dozens of different Pacific seafood species, and large tanks of crab and lobster. Food stalls overflow with everything from dried fish (used for flavouring) to glistening honey-glazed roast quail—which makes a great mid-morning snack. Keep your eyes peeled for jackfruit, an enormous tropical fruit bigger than a watermelon.

A Word of Warning – Though Chinatown itself is perfectly safe during the day, the stretch of Hastings Street west of the district is an area plagued by drug trafficking, and it's not advisable to walk through it at any time, day or night. To walk to Chinatown from downtown, it's best to take Pender Street. The intersection of Main and Hastings streets, in front of the old Carnegie Library, suffers the same problem—tread warily.

The Best of Chinatown

Dr. Sun Yat-Sen Classical Chinese Garden★ – *578 Carrall St. at Keefer St. See Parks and Gardens.* This classical Chinese garden is the district's visitor highlight, but the smaller, less developed meditation garden adjacent to it *(toward Quebec St.)* is also lovely in its own right, and there's no admission charge. Both gardens honour the father of modern China, Sun Yat-Sen (1866–1925).

Chinese Benevolent Association – **[A]** *refer to map on inside front cover.* *108 Pender St.* The association's home (1909) is a lavishly painted example of a tong headquarters—tongs being community support associations, not the pseudo-gangs as often supposed.

Chinese Cultural Centre – *555 Columbia St. 604-658-8880. www.cccvan.com.* Adjacent to the Sun Yat Sen garden, the cultural centre was founded in 1973 to foster understanding of the Chinese people and to promote Chinese culture and art. It accomplishes these goals by hosting special events, celebrations and language classes, as well as changing art exhibits. The centre also houses an evocative museum describing the painful experience of Chinese-Canadians in their new homeland and their forced imprisonment during World War II. Upstairs, you'll learn about the impressive record of Chinese-Canadians who served in the country's military.

Chinese Freemasons Building – **[B]** *refer to map on inside front cover. Northwest corner of Pender & Carrall Sts.* It is rumored that Sun Yat-Sen secretly lived in this 1907 structure when he came to Vancouver in in the early 20C. Here he plotted with the Cheekungton, a powerful Chinese secret society, to overthrow the Manchu government in China.

Sam Kee Building – **[C]** *refer to map on inside front cover. Southwest corner of Pender & Carrall Sts.* At 1.8m/6ft wide, this two-storey building claims to be the world's narrowest. It's an insurance office; a property-line dispute forced the narrow design.

Chinatown Classics

Tea is more than simply a beverage to the Chinese, and at **Ten Lee Hong Tea & Ginseng** *(500 Main St.; 604-689-7598)* you can experience a formal tea ceremony and investigate the dozens of medicinal uses for ginseng—which would truly be a miracle substance if it accomplished everything its adherents claimed it did.

Fans of Chinese cooking won't want to miss **Ming Wo** *(23 E. Pender St.; 604-683-7268; www.mingwo.com)*, a small warehouse stacked floor-to-ceiling with cookware, including the greatest variety of woks you're ever likely to see.

Chinatown Cuisine: Dim Sum

One of the many translations of this Mandarin term is "little treats"—and each serving is indeed small, and a treat. But a meal composed of a half-dozen dim sum baskets is anything but modest—baked, fried or steamed pastries, buns, cakes and dumplings are always filling and intensely flavoured. Common "packaging" materials include wheat, rice and taro flour; some dim sum arrive wrapped in banana leaves; some have no wrapping at all, like the chicken feet that fascinate—and repel—most Westerners. Fillings include shrimp, oysters, fish, squid and other seafood; pork and chicken; bean pastes and tofu; custards and fruit preparations.

Chefs arrive at the crack of dawn at dim sum restaurants to prepare the day's

selection of up to 50 types of morsels; midday diners start arriving just before noon, and the "dim sum ladies" begin trundling up and down the aisles, offering customers the chance to peek at what's in the basket or on the platter. It's best to go with friends and sample many different kinds—don't be afraid to be adventurous. Unless you're fluent in Mandarin or Cantonese, you may not always know exactly what's in each item, but there's fun in the mystery. Gourmands can take heart in the fact there are estimated to be more than 500 kinds of dim sum, with new ones being created all the time.

Floata Seafood Restaurant – *180 Keefer St. 604-602-0368. www.floata.com.* With headquarters in Hong Kong, the largest Chinese restaurant in Canada can seat 1,000 (yes, one thousand) people. Almost every table will be filled on a busy day; don't arrive late. Specialties include Peking duck, which is barbecued on-site.

Garden Villa Seafood Restaurant – *127 E. Pender St. 604-688-3877.* This inconspicuous second-floor dim-sum shrine in the heart of Chinatown specializes in shrimp, oyster and fish dumplings. Be sure to try the taro balls.

West End★

Bounded by Thurlow St., False Creek and English Bay, Stanley Park and Georgia St.

With high-rise apartments packed cheek-to-jowl along tree-lined streets, the West End is what Vancouver officials claim is the highest-density residential area in North America. The heart of the neighbourhood is **Denman Street,** a European-style artery lined with small shops, cafes and bistros. Here, fruit and vegetable vendors offer fresh produce from all climes and culinary persuasions, and local independent coffee shops compete with larger national chains (did someone say Seattle?).

The West End was the first "suburban" residential development in the young city's life—city fathers prevailed on Cornelius van Horne, the ultra-powerful nabob of the Canadian Pacific Railway, to use his influence in Ottawa to back Vancouver's plea for title to a military reserve—now Stanley Park. The park made the new West End housing development considerably more attractive. The neighbourhood's transition to high-rise apartments occurred largely in the period between World War II and 1960.

English Bay Beach★★

Beach Ave. & Denman St.

If you're in Vancouver in the winter, spring or fall months, you may wonder why the beach here looks so neatly tended, the sand raked and logs lined up back from the water. Do people really swim here? Yes, they do. In July, August and early September, English Bay's shallow water warms sufficiently to welcome all but the wimpiest souls, and by noon on sunny days, assorted families and sunbathers with towels and picnic stuff will be spread out by every log. Kayakers paddle by; kids splash in the shallows; and every once in a while, when the wake from a container ship reaches shore, intrepid body surfers hop on a break for a short ride. When you're lying on the beach with the palm gardens *(see Parks and Gardens)* behind you, it's not easy to believe you're in the homeland of ice hockey.

- **English Bay Bathhouse** offers showers and a place to change; it rents kayaks and sailboards, as well.

Gelati Break

Morning, noon or night, be sure to stop in at **Mum's Gelato** *(849 Denman St.; 604-681-1500)* to sample the dozens of Italian-style gelati and ices.

West End Markets

Capers, at 1675 Robson Street, is the city's leading natural-foods outlet, and a great place to get a sandwich for lunch *(604-687-5288)*. The **Robson Public Market** *(1610 Robson St.)* is an indoor aggregation of butchers, bakers, delis and produce vendors (no candlestick-makers) who sell everything from North European sausages to East Asian rice dishes.

Cuisines available to passersby range from fiery Korean at **Madangcoul** *(847 Denman St.; 604-688-3585)* to delectable Spanish at **Tapastree** *(1829 Robson St.; 604-606-4680; www. tapastree.ca).*

Coffee Capital

You'll notice something interesting about the intersection of Robson and Thurlow streets. On the southwest corner is a Starbucks (often visited by motorcycle riders). On the northeast corner is, yes, another Starbucks. Both stores do a thriving business. And on the northwest corner is a local coffee and pastry shop, also constantly packed. Vancouverites cede the title of most-coffee-crazed city to no one!

Roedde House Museum

1415 Barclay St. See Historic Sites.

MOWtown

With more than $1 billion of activity and more than 200 productions per year, Vancouver ranks right up there with Los Angeles, San Francisco, New York City and Toronto as a leader in North American film and video production. Because so many TV movies and series are now produced here, the city has acquired the nickname, "MOWtown," for Movie of the Week.

Popular films shot in the Vancouver area include:

Carnal Knowledge (1971)	*Legends of the Fall* (1994)	*X-Men* (2002)
First Blood (1982)	*Happy Gilmore* (1996)	*X-2: X-Men United* (2003)
The Accused (1988)	*Double Jeopardy* (1999)	*I, Robot* (2004)
Russia House (1990)	*Scooby-Doo* (2002)	*X-Men: The Last Stand* (2006)

Yaletown★

Bounded by Davie, Homer, Nelson & Cambie Sts., and Pacific Blvd.

Yaletown isn't the only former warehouse district given new life by redevelopment, but it's certainly one of the best-known and the most dynamic. What was, just 20 years ago, a decaying area dedicated to the business of produce shipping has been transformed into a bustling commercial district chockablock with hip restaurants, galleries and shops.

Long before it was a warehouse district, Yaletown was the edge of a tidal flatland. The curving brick wall in the tiny park at Mainland and Davie streets marks the shoreline of two centuries ago, before dredging and filling converted much of False Creek to dry land. That area was also the site of the Expo '86 fairgrounds, which have recently been converted into a massive housing complex called Concord Pacific Place.

It all happens along two blocks of Hamilton and Mainland streets *(between Nelson & Davie Sts.)*. Perched above these two streets, behind the loading docks that once served delivery trucks—now turned into patios and a broad promenade—are some of the city's glitziest restaurants, toniest shops and finest salons. The scene on a nice evening, when young office workers flock to the area, rivals that of Greenwich Village or Soho in New York City.

Yaletown Sampler

Here are some "musts" among Yaletown's many restaurants and shops:

Barbara Jo's Books to Cooks – *1740 West 2nd Ave. 604-688-6755. www.bookstocooks.com.*

Blue Water Cafe – *1095 Hamilton St. 604-688-8078. www.bluewatercafe.net.*

Chintz & Company – *950 Homer St. 604-689-2022. www.chintz.com.*

Cioppino's – *1133 Hamilton St. 604-688-7466. www.cioppinosyaletown.com.*

Vancouver Cigar Company – *1093 Hamilton St. 604-685-0445. www.vancouvercigar.com.*

Roundhouse Community Centre

181 Roundhouse Mews, in the Concord Pacific Place development. 604-713-1800; www.roundhouse.ca.

Once upon a time Canadian Pacific engineers used the huge turntable here to juggle locomotives and railcars. The railroad is long gone, but the turntable forms the centerpiece of the courtyard for an intriguing neighbourhood centre. Outside, a massive retired locomotive thrills kids and rail fans, while the gallery space inside features temporary shows by local artists and craftspeople. It's a worthy reminder of this now chic neighbourhood's gritty past.

Kitsilano

Bounded by Burrard St., W. 12th Ave., MacDonald St. & False Creek/English Bay.

"I've got a nice little place in Kits," is the way that thousands of Vancouverites happily explain their residences—and thousands more wish they could. Indeed, thriving, progressive Kitsilano enjoys the best reputation among all Vancouver's residential districts.

From 1966 and into the '70s, peace signs were prominent front-door insignias, a VW van was parked on almost every block, and a protest of some sort was the subject of constant telephone-pole posters. Nearby Vanier Park witnessed any number of be-ins and demonstrations, and when the entire city was virtually shut down by antiwar protests in March and April 1967, Kitsilano was the heart of the action. In the 21C, the neighbourhood still leans heartily leftward; some of those same activists are now long-term residents who have raised their families here.

Quintessential Kitsilano

Sophie's Cosmic Café
2095 West 4th Ave. 604-732-6810. www.sophiescosmiccafe.com. With its Naugahyde booths, antique-toy décor, and a menu that ranges from waffles to falafel to veggie burgers and quesadillas, Sophie's is an institution that has withstood the many tides of change running through Kitsilano. Since it opened in the 1940s, the cafe has specialized in huge breakfast plates, bowls of rich oyster stew, and deep-dish apple pie that towers seven inches high.

Banyen Books & Sound
3608 W. Fourth Ave. 604-732-7912. www.banyen.com. Here you'll find a copy of seemingly every self-help book ever written, as well as a CD inventory that includes flute music from every continent. Founded in the early 1970s, Banyen devotes itself to personal growth in a thoroughly ecumenical fashion—volumes on everything from Buddhist to Zoroastrian thought, and music ranging from Gregorian chants to Paul Winter. Banyen does a thriving business shipping its books and CDs throughout North America.

Bordering Vanier Park along the English Bay shore, Kitsilano is paradise for those who love the outdoors. Neighbourhood amenities include Kitsilano Beach, Vancouver's largest outdoor pool, sand volleyball courts, a walking/biking/in-line-skating path, and easy access to downtown—a 20-minute walk across the Burrard Bridge.

Craftsman-style Gems — You'll find some of Canada's best examples of Craftsman-style residential architecture in serene Kitsilano. The biggest and best ones are near Vanier Park *(between Chestnut & Arbutus Sts., north of Cornwall St.).*

Shaughnessy

Bounded by Granville St., West 12th Ave., Oak St. & West 33rd Ave.

This is Vancouver's original mansion district, a sublime hill where the city's first tycoons—such as timber baron H.R. MacMillan—who made their fortunes in the lumber, rail and trade industries, built stone and timber mansions in the early part of the 20C. Curving streets (the city's first) wind past palatial homes of granite and fir, with broad lawns, semicircular drives, perfectly trimmed hedges and spreading oaks and maples. Yes, it does look a bit like a baronial English neighbourhood—that's just how it was intended when it was developed by the Canadian Pacific Railway in 1907. Although this isn't the priciest real estate in the Vancouver area any more (that title goes to the West Vancouver waterfront), a drive along Shaughnessy's quiet streets still produces its share of "oohs" and "ahhs." Descendants of the original residents now share their neighbourhood with Hollywood stars who rent homes here during film shoots.

Monster Homes

Though Shaughnessy itself remains much as it was 75 years ago, the districts on either side of Granville and Oak, and to the south toward the airport, experienced a phenomenon in the mid-1990s whose result is conspicuous today. Huge, newly built, chateau-like houses crowd next to each other on small lots that once held much smaller residences. These "monster homes," as long-time Vancouverites call them, were built by wealthy immigrants from Hong Kong who came to Canada to avoid the Chinese takeover of the former British colony in 1997. Taking advantage of their Commonwealth passports, and cashing in their Asian fortunes, the new settlers purchased old houses, tore down the small buildings, and replaced them with the biggest homes building codes would allow. Ironically, many of those who fled to Vancouver before 1997 have now returned to Hong Kong.

Y ou'll recognize Vancouver's cityscape by the blue-glass and brushed-metal style of the buildings that line the waterfronts along False Creek and Coal Harbour. Most of the city's landmarks date from the 20C, as Vancouver was founded in 1886, and a ferocious fire destroyed most of it shortly after it incorporated. Whereas Gastown *(see Historic Sites)* preserves the city's pre-1900 buildings, you can see the finest examples of contemporary architectural design downtown along a one-mile loop that makes an easy walk. So put on your sneakers and sunglasses—the glare off the glass buildings on a sunny day can be fierce—and have a look at the landmarks that define this international city.

Canada Place★★

999 Canada Place Way, at the foot of Howe St. 604-775-7200. www.canadaplace.ca. Promenade open 24 hours; IMAX shows daily noon–10pm. $11.50.

You can't help but notice the white "ship" moored in Burrard Inlet. It has become, after almost a quarter-century, an icon of Vancouver. The graceful canvas "sails" of Canada Place lift 70m/230ft above the water below— and are, cynics say, a blatant rip-off of the Sydney Opera House (just as Denver International Airport is undoubtedly a

copy of Canada Place). Aside from their obvious reference to the city's lifelong connection to maritime affairs, the roof peaks, held aloft by central pillars, make room for large open areas within the city's convention centre underneath. With massive cruise ships docked alongside, the whole structure is eminently practical, no matter how fanciful it appears. Built by the federal government for Expo '86, this was Canada's pavilion during the fair. Head up to the second-level **promenade** for wonderful **views★★** of the harbour, Stanley Park and the North Shore mountains.

An **IMAX** theatre housed within shows big-screen films, whose topics range from NASCAR auto racing to Everest exploration, and the top-notch Pan-Pacific Hotel *(see Must Stay)* occupies the southwest corner of the building, next to the Vancouver World Trade Centre. A pedestrian path departs from the southwest corner to Stanley Park, which is about a 10-minute walk away.

Fast Facts

- Canada Place rests on 6,000 pilings, some of which are from a pier that has occupied this spot since the 1920s.
- A Teflon coating keeps the exterior fabric clean.

Library Square★★

350 W. Georgia St. 604-331-3603. www.vpl.Vancouver.bc.ca.

Is it a grandiose imitation of ancient architecture—or a memorable addition to the Vancouver landscape? Hardly anyone is neutral about this colourful design by famed Canadian architect Moshe Safdie. Safdie denies the building's similarities to the Roman Colosseum—but the resemblance is obvious to virtually everyone else. Made of brown pre-cast concrete, the complex opened in 1995, and houses the main Public Library, government offices, retail shops and a splendid outdoor plaza that's great for people-watching on sunny days. Naysayers who find the whole thing too much should glance across the street, at the Vancouver Post Office *(on the north side of Georgia St.)*.

Library Lowdown – The seven-level Public Library itself is one of the largest anywhere, with 1.2 million items, a large children's library, extensive audio-visual and electronic materials sections, and numerous nooks and crannies that are specifically designed to provide private reading spots. Sky bridges that span the seven-storey atrium are guaranteed to wrinkle the brows of anyone with acrophobia. The ground floors hold coffee shops, cafes and small retailers.

BC Place Stadium★

777 Pacific Blvd. 604-669-2300. www.bcplacestadium.com.

Though some have derided its appearance as a puff pastry left out too long, this fabric-dome-roofed structure has served its role admirably since 1983, and will be pressed into service during the 2010 Winter Olympics for opening and closing ceremonies, and medal presentations. (Olympic bid organizers pointed out that using BC Place would alleviate fears of rain-drenched ceremonies at a snow-sports extravaganza.) The stadium is home field for the BC Lions Canadian Football League team, and host to rock and pop concerts, car and home shows and the like. Puffed up it may be—the roof is held up by air pressure—but it nonetheless claims a solid role in Vancouver life.

BC Sports Hall of Fame and Museum★ – *In BC Place. See Musts for Kids.*

Christ Church Cathedral★

690 Burrard St. at Georgia St. 604-682-3848. www.cathedral.vancouver.bc.ca. Open before and after regularly scheduled worship services, for concerts, and for tours by appointment.

Outside, solid sandstone. Inside, massive hewn timbers bracing the roof. Though this is the seat of the Anglican diocese of Vancouver (it became a cathedral in 1929), it was built in 1889 to remind its members of parish churches back in Britain. Now it's the oldest church in the city, a holdover from a time when this was a residential neighbourhood.

Cathedral Place

[D] *refers to map on the inside front cover. 925 W. Georgia St. at Hornby St.* This 1990 office tower was expressly designed to blend with its historic companions—the copper roof and gargoyles mimic the Hotel Vancouver across Georgia Street, and the Art Deco touches reflect the 1920s building it replaced. Ground-floor stonework, meanwhile, corresponds to Christ Church Cathedral to the west.

Its steep, gabled roof, arched windows and huge stained-glass windows are architectural treasures, and the church is frequently the site of concerts and other performances, both religious and secular. Plans to demolish the cathedral and sell the land for an office tower aroused a huge controversy in the late 1970s. In the end, the Episcopal diocese sold the density rights to the land to the developers of Cathedral Place just north *(see sidebar),* allowing that building to rise taller, and gaining money for renovation of the church.

Harbour Centre Tower★

555 W. Hastings St.

Even after a quarter-century, this ungainly 167.5m/550ft landmark on West Hastings Street remains Vancouver's tallest building. The circular pod atop the tower houses a viewing platform and restaurant *(see Musts for Fun)*; you can access it via a glass-walled elevator. Astronaut Neil Armstrong officially opened the building in August 1977, leaving behind—you guessed it—a footprint.

Hotel Vancouver★

900 W. Georgia St., between Burrard & Hornby Sts. 604-684-3131. www.fairmont.com/hotelvancouver.

One of the continent-wide chain of massive, chateau-style hotels built by Canadian railroads in the late 19C and early 20C, the "Hotel Van" is a city icon. Its copper roof and gabled tower are often photographed to symbolize the city. Built by the Canadian National Railway and opened in 1939, the hotel was later taken over by Canadian Pacific; it's now operated by the Fairmont chain, which invested millions of dollars in renovations in the 1990s. Special attention was devoted to the brushed-metal and glass Art Moderne touches in the lobby, which is worth a visit just to experience the atmosphere in one of the world's landmark hotels *(see Must Stay)*.

Law Courts and Robson Square★

800 Robson St., between Hornby & Howe Sts.

Babylonian-style hanging gardens, suspended pools and waterfall freshets of this complex make it hard to grasp the fact that it is indeed a single building. And despite its aesthetic appeal, serious business does take place inside ("law courts" is a term for courthouse).

Designed by Arthur Erickson, the facility you see here today was not the one originally intended for this site. A massive 55-storey tower was planned in the early 1970s, but never realized. The hundreds of workers, visitors and residents you'll see enjoying the Law Courts' outside spaces on a sunny day can attest to the wisdom of that decision. There's also an ice rink for winter skating, and small garden patches at various levels with something in bloom virtually year-round.

Marine Building★

355 Burrard St. at Hastings.

Money was no object for the builders of this elaborate structure, who intended it to be one of the snazziest buildings in North America. Sightseers who still gawk at it agree they succeeded: the terra-cotta frieze over the entrance, the phantasmagoric "Mayan" tilework in the lobby, the massive, figured-brass elevator doors—all are palatial in colour and form and sing of a bygone day when style was as important as function (or budget). The 21-storey building was the tallest in the British Commonwealth when it opened in 1930; today it's overshadowed by modern office towers, but none can match its flair. Exterior ornamentation illustrates Vancouver's maritime history, with clipper ships and marine creatures such as sea horses crowding the entranceway frieze. The blue, green and maroon tile and brass lobby is a fanciful representation of the inside of a Mexican temple.

Building or Bust – It could be said that the whole thing was a fanciful business enterprise—the structure was finished at $2.3 million, almost 100 percent over budget. Its builders quickly went broke, and the Marine Building was sold to the Guinness family for $900,000 in 1933. A mosaic in the lobby floor depicts the Zodiac—you might say the building was born under a bad sign—in the midst of the Great Depression. Today it's a historic jewel.

Orpheum Theatre★ – *884 Granville St. See Performing Arts.*

Sun Tower

100 W. Pender St. Newspaper publisher Louis Taylor aimed for extravagance with this towering edifice. At 17 storeys, it was tallest in the British Empire for a brief two years, from 1912 to 1914; the copper dome is an example of Beaux Arts design. And the nine half-clad buxom maidens (caryatids) that adorn the top storeys, where gargoyles are usually found, were meant to prick modest Edwardian sensibilities. They did.

Eaton Building (Sears)

701 Granville St. at Robson St. 604-685-7112.

This massive 1970s building is monumental in several ways. Its bulbous, light-shaded tubular shape has earned it a nickname drawn from classic literature: the "Great White Whale." It was the downtown Eaton store until that longtime Canadian chain went bankrupt in 1999. Sears took it over, and reconfigured the Eaton retail persona, which quickly flopped. Now this is a Sears store—bigger than usual, for sure, and impossible to miss.

Eatons – The Eaton retail chain was the product of an industrious Irishman, one Timothy Eaton, who immigrated to Canada when he was 22 years old. In 1869 he opened his first department store, locating it in Toronto and offering a new incentive to customers—the money-back guarantee. Before long, he established a second store in Toronto as well as a mail-order business, and the chain spread from there. The holiday season brought wonderful mechanized displays in Eaton department store windows. In 1905, Eaton's introduced its Santa Claus Parade, which became the largest parade in North America by the 1950s, televised to a world audience of some 30 million viewers.

Vancouver as Stand-in

With a constant stream of film and TV productions in the Vancouver area, many city landmarks have served as sets for films—often standing in for other structures of various sorts. The Vancouver Art Gallery, for instance, was used as the courtroom for the key scenes in *The Accused,* in which Jodie Foster won her first Academy Award. Gastown was transformed into Helena, Montana, for *Legends of the Fall,* with Brad Pitt and Anthony Hopkins. The Hotel Vancouver's green copper roofs became European in the film *Russian Roulette*. And, of course, a West End apartment house was Agent Sculley's Washington, DC home during the eight-year run of the popular TV show *The X-Files*.

The Vancouver area landscape also serves to represent locales around the world when Hollywood comes calling. Most famously, the deep woods around Hope, at the east end of the Lower Mainland, were the setting for *First Blood,* the kick-off film in the Rambo series that helped make Sylvester Stallone an international star.

Holy Rosary Cathedral

646 Richards St. at Dunsmuir St. 604-682-6774. Open Mon–Sat 6am–6pm, Sun 7:30am–9pm.

Once the tallest fir on the early Vancouver skyline occupied this spot. Now a 66m/217ft steeple holds its place, and the 15 large stained-glass windows dapple light inside much as old-growth woods do. One of the windows (to the left of the altar) was actually made in Paris in 1896, before the church was built. The Gothic Revival-style building was finished in 1900, and declared a cathedral 16 years later. Pope John-Paul II sang Mass here in 1984; an intriguing contrast is presented by the small army of street people who spread their sleeping bags beneath the open atrium on the cathedral's south side.

Sinclair Centre

757 W. Hastings St., at Granville St. www.sinclaircentre.com.

Four historic buildings were melded into a modern shopping complex in this exemplary adaptation. The old Post Office (1910), Customs Warehouse, Federal Building and Winch Building—all imposing Edwardian stone structures—have been joined by an interior atrium-courtyard that houses shops and cafes. The 20 retail stores are boutiques in the class of Leone and Escada. Two blocks south, the modern version of the same thing is **Pacific Centre** *(700 W. Georgia St.; 604-688-7235, www.pacificcentre.ca)* an entirely underground shopping mall that stretches three city blocks north and south between Granville and Howe streets. Theoretically, guests at the Four Seasons Hotel need never go outside to shop. The mall's anchor store is Holt Renfrew, an upscale apparel chain *(604-681-3121)*, and a huge food court supplies nourishment to hungry shoppers.

The Pendulum

HSBC Building, Georgia & Hornby Sts. www.885westgeorgia.com. Shades of Edgar Allen Poe. One of the best-known pieces of public art in Vancouver, this 15m/50ft-long brushed-steel sculpture swings above the three-storey atrium lobby of the building's namesake bank. Vancouver artist Alan Storey created the piece in 1985.

Landmark Bridges

Burrard Street Bridge

Burrard St., crossing False Creek.

This six-lane 1932 span over False Creek comprises an arched gateway to downtown Vancouver. The decorative frieze on the stucco arch reads "By Land and Sea We Prosper." Stroll across the bridge at sunset to enjoy the expansive **views** of the western horizon and sundown light on the glass towers along False Creek. Residents and knowledgeable visitors use the bridge, and the south end of Burrard Street, as a shortcut to the airport and the highway to Seattle, bypassing the retail congestion of South Granville Street.

Lions Gate Bridge

North end of Stanley Park Causeway, linking Vancouver to the North Shore.

It's hard to believe, today, that this soaring structure was built with private funds. The Guinness family used proceeds from their brewing enterprises to provide access to North Shore property developments, opening the bridge in 1938. The BC government bought it for $6 million in 1963, and at the end of the 20C, the span's increasing inability to handle all the traffic spurred numerous proposals to replace or expand it—ranging from adding another deck, to building a tunnel beneath the entire downtown Vancouver peninsula. In the end, superficial improvements were made, and all other schemes abandoned.

Traffic crosses on three lanes, the centre lane reversing at midday. The bridge's main span is 472m/1,440ft, and the deck is 61m/180ft above the water. It's also called the First Narrows bridge, after the passage it crosses.

Second Narrows Bridge

On Hwy. 1, across Burrard Inlet.

This cantilevered six-lane bridge (the highway is balanced out over the water, rather than suspended from cables) was built in 1960, and spans 323m/1,060ft. During construction a part of the north arm span collapsed, killing 18 workers; in 1994 the bridge was renamed the Ironworkers Memorial Bridge. Its original name (still in common use) refers to the fact that it crosses the second neck in Burrard Inlet; the Lions Gate Bridge spans the first.

The unique history and culture of Pacific Canada are what distinguish Vancouver's best museums—Native totems and crafts, seafaring history, singular artwork that depicts the stunning BC landscape. The number of noteworthy museums in Vancouver may be modest, but you'll find collections here that you won't find anywhere else on earth.

UBC Museum of Anthropology★★★

6393 N.W. Marine Dr., on the University of British Columbia campus. 604-822-5087. www. moa.ubc.ca. Open daily mid-May–Labour Day 10am–5pm (Tue until 9pm). Rest of the year Tue–Sun 11am–5pm (Tue until 9pm). Closed Dec 24 & 25. $9.

So, you fancy totem poles? Well, you've come to the right place. Known the world over for its vast collection of aboriginal works—and the sensational building that houses them—the Museum of Anthropology (MOA) is one of North America's most important cultural institutions. It's also a great place to spend an afternoon looking at wonderful things.

Designed by Arthur Erickson, the cast-concrete building rests atop a bluff overlooking the Strait of Georgia. From the outside, its huge concrete frame mimics a First Nations longhouse. As you descend a ramp into the main gallery, the roof rises, providing ever-taller halls for the totems that form the centrepiece of the museum's collection.

Treasures of the MOA

Great Hall – The museum's main gallery boasts ground-to-ceiling glass walls that let in every bit of daylight available. Massive **totems** draw your attention first—almost all the Northwest Coast First Nations are represented, but the most prominent are the Haida, Kwakwaka'wakw, Nisga'a and Coast Salish, in whose hands the art of carving totems reached its peak in the late 19C. Ravens, whales, eagles, salmon, bears, wolves and countless other creatures carved into the cedar logs demonstrate the Native people's affinity for the natural world that sustained them.

Don't overlook the smaller pieces. Bentwood cedar boxes, plaited-reed baskets, ceremonial masks—all show the skill, subtlety and figured designs that make Northwest Coast art distinctive.

Visible Storage Galleries – You'll find one of the world's most important collections of aboriginal artifacts here. Almost half of the 35,000-item inventory is displayed in cases for visitors to see, in what the museum calls "visible storage."

Koerner Ceramics – This glistening 600-piece collection of European ceramics poses an intriguing contrast to the massive wood works just outside—both are beautiful and skillfully made, but utterly different in style.

Works by Bill Reid – The museum is also the most important repository for the work of famed Haida artist Bill Reid *(see sidebar, below)*. Reid helped create some of the poles and longhouses outside the museum in its representation of a traditional coast village. Strolling these paths, past alder groves, with totems peering down, you can almost sense the silent spirits that inhabit the coves and fjords of BC's coast. Inside, you'll find both small and large pieces, including a fine selection of Reid's jewellery, and a canoe carved in the traditional fashion, with placards showing how it was done.

Lustrous and haunting, *Raven and the First Men* is the work universally considered Reid's masterpiece. A depiction of the Haida creation myth, this sculpture has its own separate gallery at the museum. Reid carved it from a four-ton cedar block, and it was dedicated by Prince Charles in 1980. The work rests in a bed of sand brought by the Haida people from the beach in the Queen Charlotte Islands. According to Haida legend, it was on this very sand that Raven opened the clamshell in which humanity huddled, freeing the first men to discover the world.

Bill Reid

A Canadian national treasure, Bill Reid (1920–1998) is one of those artists whose work is firmly rooted in his cultural heritage but transcends it completely. The Haida are the ancestral people of the Queen Charlotte Islands, whose mist-clad, high-timbered shores evoke both the forces of nature and the spirits of vanished lifestyles. Reid was born in Victoria (his mother was Haida) and paid little attention to his heritage until he visited his grandfather in the islands in 1943. That visit fired his interest in traditional Haida carving, and he abandoned a career in radio.

Reid's 40-year life as an artist encompassed works both big—totems and canoes—and small, such as finely-wrought gold and silver jewellery. His pieces reside in collections around the world, but his fame rests on the large works he did on commission late in life. A massive sculpture of a canoe bearing the earth's creatures decorates the International Terminal at Vancouver International Airport; a breaching killer whale greets visitors to Vancouver Aquarium; and a huge wooden bear sits in the Museum of Anthropology's Great Hall.

Vancouver Art Gallery★★

750 Hornby St., at Robson St. 604-662-4719. www.vanartgallery.bc.ca. Open daily 10am–5:30pm (Tue & Thu until 9pm) & fourth Friday of every month 10am–11pm. Closed Jan 1 & Dec 25. $15.

Not only is this stately building Pacific Canada's leading art institution, it also represents the work of BC's two best-known architects, and has the largest collection of the province's most famous artist—Emily Carr *(see sidebar)*. Designed by Francis Rattenbury, who also did the Parliament Buildings in Victoria *(see Excursions)*, it served as the Vancouver Courthouse from 1911 to 1974. It was recast in 1983 as an art museum by Arthur Erickson, who transformed the rotunda into a core of light along the centre of the building. Hung here are works by modern BC artists such as Jack Shadbolt. The lower floors hold temporary and travelling exhibits; the third floor is the home of the museum's large collection of works by Carr, which is its greatest distinction.

Grounds for Dissension – The museum grounds are as dynamic as the art inside. Various parts of the building and its plaza and fountains outside have served as the settings for innumerable films. The steps on the southwest corner, facing Robson, are ground zero for protests in Western Canada—virtually no topic is too trifling for someone to set up a soapbox here; major controversies draw hundreds of demonstrators.

Emily Carr

Born in Victoria, Emily Carr (1871–1945) found her greatest success in the more cosmopolitan Vancouver, where she lived for a while as a young woman, and formed her lifelong disdain for artistic and social convention. The city's art museum was one of the few institutions to show her work during her lifetime, so when Carr died she willed almost all her works to the Art Gallery, which hangs a rotating selection of about two dozen canvases.

Carr's brooding, dark-hued portraits of her homeland's rain forests, and the vanishing aboriginal life within them, are so distinctive that her paintings are instantly recognisable. Much of her work depicts First Nations life and draws its style from that motif—*Big Raven*, for instance, resembles the raven's representations on totem poles. Carr is often classed with Frida Kahlo and Georgia O'Keeffe, artists with whom she shared both personal and cultural perspectives.

Vancouver Maritime Museum★★

1905 Ogden Ave., Vanier Park. 604-257-8300. www.vancouvermaritimemuseum.bc.ca.
Open Victoria Day–Labour Day daily 10am–5pm. Rest of the year Tue–Sat 10am-5pm,
Sun noon–5 pm. $10.

Vancouver's museum devoted to its maritime history sits, appropriately, on the shoreline at the entrance to False Creek. It offers an intriguing survey of the boats that plied the Northwest Coast, the people who sailed them and the reasons they did so. The museum was built as a BC centennial project in 1958.

St. Roch – The tentlike roof of the building shields the mast of a Royal Canadian Mounted Police patrol ship that was first to traverse the Northwest Passage through Canada's Arctic in both directions. Amazingly enough, despite its career bashing through icy waters, the *St. Roch* is a wood-hulled boat—and a small one, at just 32m/104ft, built in a Vancouver shipyard in 1928. The schooner is permanently dry-docked inside the museum. You can clamber into and through the ship, marveling at the incredibly tight quarters its 10-man crew occupied while battling the Arctic during the ship's unprecedented World War II voyages. The first of these trips, from Vancouver to Halifax, took two years (1940–1942), during which the ship was twice trapped in sea ice.

Exploration History – In the rest of the museum, you'll discover Vancouver's lifelong ties to maritime affairs, from the canoes carved out of cedar by Native peoples to the late-18C Northwest voyages of European explorers. Ship models and descriptive exhibits and installations (the forecastle of a sailing ship, Captain George Vancouver's *Discovery*) illustrate often-rugged life at sea.

Shipping Today – A tugboat pilothouse represents present-day seafaring; the tug's wheel stands ready for kids to turn. Exhibits explain the modern operations of Canada's busiest port.

Centennial Pole

In a small plaza south of the Maritime Museum, Vanier Park.
Not only is this majestic totem one of the finest works of famed carver Chief Mungo Martin (1879–1962), it was once the world's tallest. Martin carved it for the BC centennial in 1958, at which time the 30.5m/100ft pole reigned supreme. It was later superseded by a pole in Victoria, which was in turn surpassed by a pole erected in 2002 in Alert Bay, at the north end of Vancouver Island. The 10 clan symbols on the Centennial Pole depict the 10 bands of Martin's Kwakwaka'wakw people.

Vancouver Museum★★

1100 Chestnut St., in Vanier Park. 604-736-4431. www.vanmuseum.bc.ca. Open daily 10am–5pm (Thu until 9pm). Closed Dec 25. $10.

You'll recognise the city's oldest museum by the huge stainless-steel crab that stands in front of the entrance. Don't worry, it's harmless; sculptor George Norris fashioned the crab to symbolize the creature that guards the harbour according to First Nations lore.

Inside, the city's Native traditions and modern history come to life through a collection of more than 100,000 items, ranging from First Nations ceremonial masks to 5,500 toy soldiers to neon signs from Vancouver's heyday as a world capital of this commercial art. Founded in 1894, the Vancouver Museum now shares a complex with the **H.R. MacMillan Space Centre★** *(see Musts for Kids);* the building's cone-shaped roof mimics a Salish cedar rain-hat.

Exploration and Settlement Galleries – Vancouver's history is a 200-year tale of Native habitation, European exploration, early timber harvesting, and the city's growth into a trade and business centre. Each period is illustrated in this walk-through collection of dioramas, with massive saw blades, huge timbers, a general store, clipper ship artifacts, and mementos of Expo '86.

Vancouver's Melting Pot – All of Vancouver's many peoples are represented, too, from the original Coast Salish inhabitants to the modern-day immigrants from Asia who have given the city its Pan-Pacific flair. An impressive collection of First Nations regalia includes ceremonial masks and button blankets.

Vancouver Stories – The museum's distinctive, walk-through Vancouver Stories galleries span the city's early development through the 1960s—a time of great political upheaval in the city—1970s and 1980s. Artifacts of the period, photos and documentary material illustrate what life was like during those decades.

Gallery Talks

For the price of admission you can accompany museum curators or historians around the museum for special gallery talks. These in-depth tours focus on specific aspects of Vancouver's past, such as the role women played in shaping the city, and the music industry in Vancouver. It all happens on Sundays at 1:30pm.

H.R. MacMillan Space Centre★ – See Musts for Kids.

Granville Island Museums

1502 Duranleau St., Granville Island. 604-683-1939. www.granvilleislandmuseums.com. Open May–Sept daily 10am–5:30pm; rest of year closed Mondays. $7.50.

Popular with residents and visitors alike, **Granville Island★** *(see Musts for Fun)* holds two small special-interest museums. You don't have to have a passion for trains or ships to enjoy a jaunt through these two closely linked attractions. The Model Train Museum and Model Ship Museum share a building, large collections, and a mission to shed light on several somewhat obscure areas of human fascination

Model Trains

This museum's collection of model trains is, believe it or not, the largest on earth, and includes almost 1,000 feet of track in the upstairs diorama. The museum's train displays reproduce every detail of huge rail yards and attest to the skill, artistry and above all, patience, that people apply to what some consider just hobbies.

Model Ships

With a focus on coastal working vessels, the model ships have all been created by British Columbia craftspeople. Some are faithful models of clipper ships with thousands of tiny parts, representing years of dedicated work by their creators.

Historic Sites

Historic site or venerable landmark? Considering Vancouver's colourful history, it's sometimes hard to categorize. We've included a few historic must-sees here, but check out the Landmarks section for more great places with a past.

Gastown★

Water St., between Carrall & Richards Sts.

Vancouver's original site is now a historic district with a split personality: housed in a fine collection of 19C buildings is a hodge-podge of 20C curio shops, art galleries, restaurants and stores. The city's first timber mills began cutting wood here from nearby forests in 1862; many of the brick and stone buildings in Gastown incorporate superstructures of old-growth Douglas fir timbers. Rundown and slated for "urban renewal" by the 1950s, the area was revived and renovated thanks to citizen activism in the early 1970s. The provincial government designated Gastown a historic district in 1971.

"Gassy" Jack Deighton

Pioneer life stories have a tendency to be colourful, and Gassy Jack's is no exception. Born in 1830 in England, Jack Deighton went to sea at 14, and eventually wound up in the new colony of British Columbia, where he opened a saloon in New Westminster, up the Fraser River from present-day Vancouver. When that failed, he loaded a canoe with a bottle of whisky, a few sticks of furniture and a yellow dog (as he later told the tale) and paddled to Burrard Inlet, where he began selling whisky to loggers at the new mill. In 1867 thirsty loggers helped him build the Globe Saloon—in 24 hours as legend has it—and Deighton's bar thrived. His nickname? Supposedly it refers to his never-failing willingness to tell a tale. Now it lives forever in the neighbourhood's moniker.

A statue of Deighton stands in Maple Tree Square at Carrall and Water Streets. Walking tours of Gastown leave from the square *(daily 2pm mid-June–Aug; 604-683-5650)*.

Steam Clock

One of the most-photographed icons in Vancouver, this clock may look historic—indeed its mechanism harks back to the early Victorian era when steam powered all machinery—yet the Gastown clock is a modern artifact. It was built in 1977, representing a capstone to the district's restoration. The whistle, which sounds every quarter-hour, is steam-driven, but the clock is electric.

Notable Buildings in Gastown

Byrnes Block – *Water St., between Carrall & Abbott Sts.* An 1886 brick edifice decked out with pediments and pilasters, this block-long structure has several distinctions—it was one of the city's first brick buildings, and it occupies the site on which "Gassy" Jack Deighton built his second saloon.

Gaolers Mews – *Water & Carrall Sts.* Across Water Street, the 19C customs house and jail now houses several Native art galleries.

Hotel Europe – *Carrall & Water Sts., east of Maple Tree Square.* This 1908 poured-concrete structure is one of the first of its kind in North America. All modern construction is required to blend with the district's heritage buildings.

Roedde House Museum

Barclay & Broughton Sts., West End. 604-684-7040. www.roeddehouse.org. Open for tours year-round Wed–Fri 2pm–4pm & Sun 2pm–4 pm; call for longer hours and special occasions during summer. $5; $6 for Sunday afternoon tea.

Quiet one-block **Barclay Heritage Square** and the neighbourhood surrounding it hint at the genteel quality of life that existed in Vancouver's West End a century ago. The highlight of this area is the opulent, fully restored 1893 Queen Anne Revival-style mansion, Roedde House. Built for Vancouver bookbinder Gustav Roedde, the house is thought to have been designed by Francis Rattenbury, the architect responsible for the Parliament Buildings and the Empress Hotel in Victoria *(see Excursions).* The home's most distinctive feature

is its rooftop **cupola**. It was from here, at the end of the 19C, that residents could watch the sea lanes for incoming vessels. Now, alas, West End development has blocked the view.

In the adjacent park you'll find a **Victorian garden;** visit in spring *(Mar–Jun)* to see the blooms of dozens of mature rhododendrons cascade down the huge bushes like coloured waterfalls.

History On Tour

Wondering where the waterfront used to be in Yaletown, or why Francis Rattenbury had to hastily leave BC for England despite his fame as an architect? To learn the answer to these and other mysteries of history, take one of the free guided walking tours of Vancouver's neighbourhoods offered by the Architectural Institute of BC in summer *(604-683-8588; www.aibc.bc.ca).*

At one end of downtown Vancouver, horse-drawn carriages trundle visitors sedately through the peaceful woods of Stanley Park. At the other end, hockey players and pucks rocket across the ice in one of the most dynamic sports of all. The opportunities for fun in Vancouver are as diverse as the city itself—and they're available year-round.

Granville Island★

On False Creek. Follow Granville Street south from downtown, then follow signs to loop back around under Granville bridge on W. 2nd Ave. Access also via ferry (see sidebar, below). 604-666-6655. www.granvilleisland.com.

A thrumming industrial zone in the period between the two world wars, then a run-down collection of warehouses, Granville Island was transformed into an effervescent district of shops, stalls, galleries and cafes in the 1970s. Today it's a heritage area operated by Parks Canada, a favourite of visitors and residents alike—especially the Public Market, where fresh foods abound, a dozen cultures mix, and the variety of smells, flavours, sights and sounds is a feast for the senses. Included in the cosmopolitan mix is a still-humming cement plant that testifies to the island's industrial past.

The island fills 12ha/29 acres with attractions; the place to start is the Granville Island information kiosk, at Johnston and Cartwright streets *(604-666-5784)*. Maps are available to guide you around the island, and the bulletin board is a colourful menu of the goings-on in the community.

Getting to Granville Island

Aquabus: 604-689-5858; www.aquabus.bc.ca. False Creek Ferries: 604-684-7781; www.granvilleislandferries.bc.ca.

The droll water taxis that ply False Creek like little jitneys are not only colourful and quaint—they're a mighty handy way to get around the area, running from lower Granville and Burrard streets to Granville Island, Vanier Park, Science World, English

Bay Bathhouse and several other locales. Rides cost $2.50–$5, depending on your destination; the companies' docks are easy to spot along the waterfront (if not, consult a tourist map). The schedule is simple: boats putter back and forth, dropping off passengers at their destinations, and veering into the dock when they see someone waiting for a pickup. Water taxis start running about 7am, and continue until 7:30pm (Aquabus) and as late as 9pm (False Creek Ferries).

Granville Island Public Market★

Granville Island; for access, see sidebar p 56. 604-666-6477. www.granvilleisland.com.
Open year-round daily 9am–7pm. Closed Jan 1 & Dec 24–25.

A large, hangar-like building right along False Creek, the Public Market is the most-visited and best-loved facility on the island. Here you can wander among dozens of independent stalls whose offerings embrace a cosmically broad range: artisan cheese and bread, seafood, fresh BC fruits and vegetables, condiments, jams and preserves, handmade sausages, butcher-block meats, crafts, and artwork. It's impossible to buy nothing.

Stalls that surround the two food courts offer a world of cuisines, including Russian, American, Chinese, Thai, Austrian and Greek. At **Stock Market** *(604-687-2433)*, cooks brew up pots of fresh soup; ladled into a bowl with a hunk of bread, this combination makes a splendid cool-season lunch. Noodles in the salads at **Zara's Pasta Deli** *(604-683-2935)* are made fresh every morning, and **Kaisereck Deli** *(604-685-8810)* piles hearty meats and cheeses on thick, dense bread. If you need a beverage to complement your lunch, **Okanagan Wine Shop** *(604-684-3364)* boasts a large inventory of BC vintages.

Must-Stop Shops

Apart from the market, the rest of the island is a gathering of tin-sided warehouses that hold galleries and shops. At **BC Wood Co-op** *(1592 Johnston St.; 604-408-2553; www.thewoodco-op.com)*, artisans transform the province's wealth of timber into beautiful furnishings. **Eagle Spirit Gallery** *(1803 Maritime Mews; 604-801-5205; www.eaglespiritgallery.com)* has a small but stunning collection of First Nations masks.

The Granville Island Brewing Company

1441 Cartwright St. 604-687-2739. www.gib.ca.

This was the first microbrewery in Canada. Though its major production facilities, having outgrown this site, have been moved to the suburbs, small batches are still brewed here, and tours and tastings are regular events. You can vote your opinion of the experimental brews.

Vancouver Lookout at Harbour Centre Tower★

555 W. Hastings St. 604-689-0421. www.vancouverlookout.com. Open May–Oct daily 8:30am–10:30pm. Rest of the year daily 9am–9pm. $11.

Though the view from this tower-topping, circular observation deck is expansive—it's the highest point in Vancouver—the ride up is what many visitors remember most. The glass-enclosed elevator soars 167.5m/550ft up the outside of the building, so it's not a good choice for anyone with severe vertigo. Once you're up top, you have a 360-degree **view★★★** of the city, with handy signs that mark everything you see.

Stanley Park Carriage Tours

Near Stanley Park information kiosk, Stanley Park Dr. 604-681-5115. www.stanleypark-tours.com. Tours depart every 20 minutes, year-round daily 9:40am–5pm. $23.36 for the basic tour. For more information about Stanley Park, see Parks and Gardens.

The clip-clop of horseshoes is a much better background sound for a tour of the park than engine RPMs. This long-established company offers group tours in horse-drawn wagons, with narration to describe the sights along the way.

Pirates for a Day

For a day on the water, rent a motor boat from **Sewell's Marina** at Horseshoe Bay *(6409 Bay St., West Vancouver. 604-921-3474, www.sewellsmarina.com. A 17-ft 60HP for 6 people is $182 for 4 hrs).* The waters of Howe Sound are usually calm, so pack a picnic lunch and let the kids pretend they are pirates while exploring the many islands and coves. The view from the water lets you see the normally-hidden luxury homes along the coastline near Lion's Bay, including the one used as Baltair's house in the BattleStar Galactica television series.

More intimate tours in private carriages, as in New York's Central Park, are available by reservation. The company provides shuttle service to its starting points, so you don't have to fight the parking wars along the park's roads.

Just for Sport

Though Vancouver's NBA team departed for, of all places, Memphis, Tennessee, the city's two remaining major-league sports franchises are quintessentially Canadian and receive heartfelt (culturally and fiscally) community support. Both the Canucks NHL team and the BC Lions CFL team have made trips to their sport's championships—Vancouver's headiest sporting moment may well have been when the Stanley Cup finals were in town in 1994. The Canucks lost the title in the waning minutes of the seventh and final game, an emotion-charged moment still talked about by residents. That same year, the Lions provided some solace by winning the Grey Cup, the CFL title. Both teams have made fairly regular trips back to the playoffs in succeeding years. Here's information on how you can take in a game during the season:

Vancouver Canucks — *General Motors Place, between the Dunsmuir & Georgia St. viaducts. 604-899-4610. www.canucks.com. Tickets $32–$94. Season: Oct–Jun.* One of North America's most popular professional sports, hockey is central to Canadian life—millions of Canadians have grown up playing pick-up games on frozen lakes. Seats sell out for most of the Canucks' home games, which are boisterous events.

BC Lions *BC Place Stadium, /// Pacific Blvd. 604-661-3626. www.bclions.com. Tickets $25. Season: Jun–Oct.* Canadian football has just three downs (as opposed to four in the States), is played on a longer and wider field, and has more scoring opportunities. Canadians believe it is thus a much more exciting game than American football.

Set Pieces

Though *The X-Files* brought Vancouver new prominence, the city has long been a film industry magnet—and it remains so, with more than $1 billion in TV and film production a year in BC. There is literally never a day that a production isn't shooting somewhere in or around Vancouver—Stanley Park, the Art Gallery grounds, Gastown and Yaletown are common settings. You are quite likely to encounter a film shoot by chance, but you can refine the process considerably by contacting the BC Film Commission for a list of current productions and locations *(BC Film Commission, 201-865 Hornby St.; 604-660-2732; www.bcfilmcommission.com)*.

Please bear in mind that, among other things, the industry likes Vancouver because city residents believe in practicing simple courtesy with stars: It's fine to watch them, but not to invade their privacy.

Snowcapped mountains, glistening blue water and serene green forests beckon everywhere you look in and around Vancouver, so it's no surprise that opportunities for outdoor recreation are practically infinite. The list includes sailing, swimming, skating, biking, in-line skating, skiing, snowshoeing, kayaking, canoeing—and that's just for starters. The city is known as a place where you can ski, sail and golf all in the same day, and energetic souls have done exactly that. A more mellow (and rational) approach is to spread the adventures out a bit. Skiing one day, kayaking the next, biking around Stanley Park after that—there's no chance you'll run out of things to do.

Harbour Cruises★

1 N. Denman St., in Coal Harbour. 604-688-7246 or 800-663-1500. www.boatcruises.com. $25–$70. Call for schedule.

Spectacular as Vancouver is from almost any angle, the most sensational way to see the cityscape is from the water that encircles it. Harbour cruises are hour-long narrated tours of the harbour; luncheon cruises head up Indian Arm, the mountain-ringed fjord just northeast of Burrard Inlet; and sunset dinner cruises run from Burrard Inlet over to English Bay, and out into the Georgia Strait and back. You won't easily forget the sight of Vancouver's skyscrapers backlit by the sun dropping over Vancouver Island; the perspective gained by being on the water adds greatly to your understanding of what is, after all, a maritime world capital.

In The Swim

Yes, Vancouver has swimming weather—three good months of it, from early July to mid-September—and the city's two major outdoor pools draw throngs on sunny days.

Pool at Second Beach – *Stanley Park Dr. 604-257-8371. $4.85.* Located in the southwest part of Stanley Park, Second Beach pool once held unheated salt-water. Now filled with heated freshwater and outfitted with slides for kids, the pool still enjoys fresh breezes off English Bay.

Kitsilano Pool – *2305 Cornwall Ave. 604-731-0011. $4.85.* Directly across the bay, at the intersection of Arbutus and Cornwall streets, the famed Kitsilano pool is the largest saltwater pool in Canada—and it's even heated.

Just Beachy

Vancouver's 12.5km/11mi of beaches not only are scenic, they offer a distinct variety of things to do. Sorry, no dogs or alcohol allowed. *Lifeguards on duty May 22–Sept 6 daily 11:30am–9pm. For information, call 604-738-8535 (mid-May–mid-Sept).*

English Bay Beach★★ – *Beach Ave. at Denman St.* A great place to swim, kayak, picnic and people-watch.

Third Beach★ – *West side of Stanley Park.* One of Stanley Park's two beaches, Third Beach is popular with locals who come to swim and sunbathe.

Jericho Beach – *West end of Point Grey Rd.* Go fly a kite, enjoy a sunset or fish off the pier here.

Kitsilano Beach – *North end of Yew St. at the waterfront.* Kitsilano's neighbourhood beach and volleyball courts are magnets for sun worshippers.

. . . And if you're interested in an all-over tan, **Wreck Beach** is Canada's most popular nude beach *(steps lead to beach near the intersection of N.W. Marine Dr. & University Blvd., west of UBC campus).*

Kayaking English Bay

Ecomarine Ocean Kayak Centre is located at the English Bay Bathhouse, 1750 Beach Ave. 604-689-7575. www.ecomarine.com. Early Jun–Labour Day Mon–Fri 11am–dusk, Sat–Sun 9am–dusk. $34 for two hours.

Sea lions and harbour seals pop their heads above water to inspect you. Lovers stroll by on the Stanley Park seawall, oblivious to your presence. The salt tang of the air clears your head, and the insistent tug of the tide competes with the gentle roll of the swells to pull you this way and that. Ocean kayaking is a sensory pleasure anywhere—in Vancouver, following the south Stanley Park shoreline, it's a wholly unexpected urban adventure.

Ecomarine rents single and double kayaks from its post in the English Bay Bathhouse; if you don't venture out into the sea lanes, little experience is needed. Third Beach is the best destination, where you can haul out on the warm sand for a picnic lunch before you head back in.

Go Fishing

If you thought that salmon fishing was verboten, you haven't heard the whole story. True, some species and runs of specific types of salmon are threatened—but others are thriving. In an average year, the Fraser River draws up to 7 million salmon returning to spawn. Federal saltwater fisheries' managers monitor salmon stocks closely to set seasons and catch limits, and plenty of opportunity remains for visitors to go salmon fishing.

Many charter operators these days encourage their clients to practice catch-and-release, but you can also have your fish frozen and shipped home. Seasons vary among species, but there is some kind of fishing available virtually year-round. Most of Vancouver's charter fleet operates out of the marina at Granville Island. Rates vary widely *(from $75– $550/person)*, depending on the duration of the trip, number of people and distance travelled.

• In Vancouver, **Bites-on Salmon Charters** *(877-688-2483, www.bites-on.com)* offers trips that leave from downtown.

The Lower Mainland still has an active commercial fishery, too. Wander by the **False Creek Fishermen's Wharf** *(east end of W. 1st Ave., just west of Granville Island)* to see (and buy) the fresh catch of the day, which might range from crab and shrimp to salmon and octopus.

Pacific Salmon

Born in freshwater streams and rivers, sometimes hundreds of miles from the sea, salmon migrate to the sea to mature. After two or more years growing in the ocean, they return to the stream of their birth to spawn and (usually) die. There are five types of Pacific salmon—chinook (king), coho (silver), sockeye (red), pink (humpy) and chum. Steelhead is a type of trout that also migrates to sea and returns to freshwater to spawn, sometimes more than once. Some salmon reach magnificent size, more than 22.6kg/50 pounds. Unfortunately, many races in lower BC and in the US face survival challenges, chiefly from overfishing and habitat destruction.

The Vancouver Aquarium *(see Musts for Kids)* in Stanly Park has created a salmon spawning stream, which runs a mere 91m/300ft from Coal Harbour up to the grounds of the aquarium. Fish first stocked here in the late 1990s have established active runs that return to spawn each October.

Watching Wildlife

The huge and stunning wilderness that surrounds Vancouver holds a healthy array of wild creatures, ranging from tidepool anemones to gargantuan whales. Almost all have been subjected to consumptive use in the past, but legal and social changes are quickly shifting the most popular wildlife activity from harvesting it to watching it. You can see plenty of wild animals—from squirrels to harbour seals—simply by strolling through Stanley Park, but the more exotic species are the subjects of guided trips that delight tens of thousands of visitors every year. In BC, whale-, eagle- and bear-watching lead the list. The first two are accessible from Vancouver; bear-watching tours require overnight travel from Vancouver *(contact Tourism BC; see Practical Information)*.

Whales – Despite the fact that over the centuries whalers have nearly harpooned them to extinction, more than 20,000 gray whales still ply the migration route between the Bering Sea and Mexico each spring and winter. Gray whales and orcas—three pods (family groups) of which inhabit Georgia Strait and Puget Sound—can both be seen on day trips that depart from Vancouver. Most charter operators depart from Victoria *(see Excursions)*, but **Vancouver Whale Watch** runs shuttles from downtown to its dock in Richmond. Daily departures *(Apr–Oct)* utilize Zodiac-type vessels, and on all trips naturalists are onboard *(604-274-9565; www. vancouverwhalewatch.com)*.

Bald Eagles – The largest concentration of bald eagles in North America returns every winter *(late Nov–Feb)* to the Squamish River, an hour north of Vancouver, to feed on a rare winter salmon run. As many as 3,700 eagles roost in the cottonwoods along the river. **Canadian Outback Adventure Company** leads raft float trips down the river to view the eagles. The mountain-rimmed valley makes a beautiful setting in which to see the birds *(604-921-7250; www. canadianoutback.com; fee includes transportation from downtown hotels)*.

Fast Facts About Whales

- Like all mammals, whales are warm-blooded, breathe air, and maintain a constant body temperature.
- Gray whales *(Eschrichtius robustus)* make the longest seasonal migration of any whales, travelling about 20,000km/12,500mi each year.
- Orcas *(Orcinus orca)*, or killer whales, are actually a type of dolphin.
- Bigger than any dinosaur, the blue whale *(Balaenoptera musculus)* is the largest animal ever to inhabit the earth. A blue whale can grow up to 34m/110ft long and weigh as much as 180,000kg/174 tons.

Musts for Kids

Sandy beaches, majestic forests, snowy mountains and hundreds of small parks and play areas—not to mention a world-class aquarium and several interactive museums—make Vancouver a superlatively kid-friendly place. Though the formal attractions for children are excellent, don't forget that a short walk along the shoreline seawall to look for seals will delight your little ones as well.

Stanley Park★★★ for Kids

Northwest end of downtown. See Parks and Gardens.

Stanley Park is the undisputed capital for young fun in Vancouver. The park's pleasures can be as simple as stopping to watch squirrels play, or building sand castles at one of its three beaches. Star of Stanley Park, the Vancouver Aquarium is a facility that will entertain the entire family.

Vancouver Aquarium★★

Southeast corner of Stanley Park, at Avison Way. 604-659-3474. www.vanaqua.org. Open late-Jun–Labour Day 9:30am–7pm; rest of the year daily 9:30am–5pm. $18.50 adults, $10.95 children.

A day here is not just fun—it's good for the world we live in. The Vancouver Aquarium has become one of the leading conservation enterprises in North America. The beautiful and exotic sea creatures it introduces to thousands of awe-struck humans are almost all threatened in some way, and the aquarium works hard to help them survive and to help us understand what that entails.

Superbly athletic marine mammals entertain the hundreds of delighted spectators who ring the arena pool. Sea otters frolic with balls in their enclosures. Trainers step into tropical exhibits to toss food to the crocodiles (one of the most popular daily events here). But throughout, the emphasis is on explaining the habitat needs, daily lives and ecological significance of the animals to encourage support for conservation.

The aquarium's famed orcas are gone, having died of old age or been sent to other marine parks, and daily shows now draw audiences with beluga whales—an exotic species for which the aquarium is one of the world's leading advocacy and research institutions. And while the shows are hugely entertaining, the "acts" are drawn from beluga real life: when one of the whales pokes its head above the surface to spout water all over a trainer (kids take great delight in this), it represents a behaviour belugas use to dislodge food from the floor of their home waters in the Arctic.

Close Encounters of the Fishy Kind

Check schedules for feedings and show times when you buy your ticket.

Amazon Gallery – This indoor wing has caimans, crocodiles, anacondas, piranhas and the world's largest freshwater fish, a type of gar that grows to 3.6m/12ft in length. Don't miss the daily crocodile feedings.

Pacific Canada – This large new wing depicts the rich and colourful marine environment along the BC coast, down to the surging tides that wash and nurture orange sunflower starfish, chartreuse sea anemones, and delicate cream-coloured nudibranchs.

Pacific Dolphins – Trainers guide these acrobatic animals through an educational show designed to demonstrate how their talents—such as their unparalleled ability to leap high out of the water—aid their lifestyles in the wild.

Seals and Friends – Frisky sea otters, harbour seals and Steller sea lions are almost always frolicking in their nearby naturalistic outdoor habitats. For a special treat, come by at feeding time.

Just for Kids

Ever wanted to spend the night with a shark? You can, in a manner of speaking, during the Vancouver Aquarium's "sleepovers," when kids get to spend the night in sleeping bags among the galleries. Or have a "beluga encounter" and go behind the scenes to feed these charming creatures, experience their unique communication style, and even pat their tongues. At Clownfish Cove play area, tots can dress up as their favourite sea creatures.

Miniature Railway and Children's Farmyard

West of Vancouver Aquarium. 604-257-8531. www.city.vancouver.bc.ca/parks/parks/stanley. Open Jun–Sept daily 10:30am–5pm. Mar–May weekends & holidays 11am–4pm. $5.50 adults, $2.75 children.

In 1886, Canadian Pacific locomotive No. 374 pulled into the Vancouver railyards, completing the first train transit of Canada. The engine pulling the Stanley Park miniature train is an exact replica of Engine 374, a fact that means more to the adults than to the kids they accompany on the train. Children just enjoy the 15-minute ride through the towering cedars and firs along the small rise in the park.

In the adjacent **farmyard,** kids can pet the tamer types among sheep, goats, pigs, cows, chickens, ducks, and a llama.

BC Sports Hall of Fame and Museum★

777 Pacific Blvd., in BC Place Stadium. 604-687-5520. www.bcsportshalloffame.com.
Open daily 10am–5pm. $8 adults, $6 children.

Sport in BC stretches a long way back, to the war canoe races First Nations residents held so seriously two centuries ago. Packed exhibit galleries in this comprehensive museum leave virtually nothing out, from the snowshoe races prospectors held for entertainment, to the stunning victory in the 1998 Olympics by Whistler resident Ross Rebagliati. He won the first snowboard gold medal ever, and became a lifetime hero to Canadians as a result. Kids who wander these halls, peering upward at sports legends past and present, are bound to develop an inclination toward one sport or another—they're all here, from curling to lacrosse.

H.R. MacMillan Space Centre★

1100 Chestnut St., in Vanier Park. 604-738-7827. www.hrmacmillanspacecentre.com.
Open year-round Tue–Sun & holidays 10am–5pm. $14 adults, $10.75 children.

Located next to the Vancouver Museum, this facility crams a lot into a small space—rather like a space station itself. Exhibits explain the basics of planetary orbits, the nature of galaxies and the history of human space exploration.
A special section delineates Canadian contributions to the latter. The two highlights are a motion simulator, which takes a virtual trip to Mars, the moon,

or some other extraterrestrial locale; and a compact planetarium where laser light shows are wedded to pop music by the eternally popular Pink Floyd, or Canadian stars such as Avril Lavigne.

Vancouver International Children's Festival

Vanier Park, late May. 604-708-5655. www.childrensfestival.ca.

This old-fashioned fair delights kids as much today as it did when it began 27 years ago. Tents and playgrounds are set up in the park south of False Creek for the weekend affair, designed to entertain whole families. Mimes, jugglers, clowns and singers stroll the grounds; puppet shows and children's plays take place on the various stages. Cotton candy, hot dogs, lemonade, a petting zoo, stilt-walkers, sack races—there's something for everyone at the world's biggest children's festival.

Maplewood Farm

405 Seymour River Pl., North Vancouver. 604-929-5610. www.maplewoodfarm.bc.ca. Open May–mid-Sept daily 10am–4pm; rest of year Tue–Sun 10am–4pm. Closed Dec 25. $4.75 adults, $2.75 children.

Why do pigs wallow in the mud, and goats like to butt heads? You'll learn the answer to these questions and more at this once-thriving dairy farm, the last surviving agricultural enterprise on the North Shore when the regional Parks Board took it over to save it from development. Maplewood occupies a pastoral, tree-shaded spot along a creek, and it's hard to tell who's happier in its bounds—the 200 domestic animals and birds that live there, or the hundreds of kids who visit on sunny days. Ponies, goats, sheep, cows, ducks and geese, squealing pigs—they're all well used to the intense attention children pay them.

Science World BC

1455 Quebec St. 604-443-7443. www.scienceworld.bc.ca. Open year-round daily 10am–6pm. $14.50 adults, $10 children. Separate fee for the Omnimax theatre.

This spherical geodesic dome perched at the end of False Creek may be the last exhibit remaining from Expo '86, but it's much more than that today. An astounding selection of interactive exhibits awaits kids inside what is affectionately known as the "golf ball." Geology, physics, electronics, biology, marine studies, zoology, physiology—hardly any scientific discipline is overlooked. Use synthesizers to make music; create a square bubble; generate plasma and electric charges; watch waves sweep the ocean floor.

The niftiest way to get to Science World is on the Aquabus, the colourful little tubs that ply False Creek *(see Musts for Fun)*.

Granville Island Children's Market

Granville Island. Follow Granville St. south from downtown, then follow signs to loop back around under Granville bridge on W. 2nd Ave. Access also via ferry (see Musts for Fun). 604-689-8477. www.kidsmarket.ca. Open year-round daily 10am–6pm.

"Daddy, may I have that?" Be prepared to hear that plea dozens of times at this aggregation of stores at the entrance to Granville Island. The multicoloured building holds a half-dozen shops selling everything from model trains to games to dolls, in greater quantity and variety than you're likely to find anywhere else in town. The shops emphasize items handmade by local artisans, and de-emphasize games and toys that are violent.

Sure, Vancouver is a centre for the film and broadcast industry, but it's also a breeding ground for Canadian music. Stars who have begun or grown their careers here include actor Michael J. Fox, singers Diana Krall, Bryan Adams and Sarah McLachlan, and famed classical pianist Jon Kimura Parker. Among symphony, opera, drama and dance, culture vultures will find plenty of performances to keep them clapping in Vancouver.

Orpheum Theatre★

884 Granville St. 604-665-3035. Box office open Mon–Fri 1pm–5pm.

The Orpheum is a one-of-a-kind arts palace from the era when the sky was the limit for theatre design. Opened in 1927, the 2,800-seat hall was once the largest theatre in Canada. Interior arches, columns and moldings of travertine, marble, stone and plaster are designed in Spanish Baroque style by architect Marcus Priteca. Converted to a movie theatre, it was scheduled to be divided up until community pressure in the mid-1970s spurred the city to buy the building and renovate it for use by the symphony. Today the theatre is once again a glittering performance palace with few equals. The original pipe organ still plays in half a dozen symphony concerts each year.

Arts Club Theatre

Granville Island, 1585 Johnston St. 604-687-5315. www.artsclub.com.

This busy and successful nonprofit theatre company is the one from which Michael J. Fox embarked on his TV and film career. It now runs productions on three stages, two on Granville Island and one at the Stanley Theatre *(see p 69)*. The company's offerings range from avant-garde drama to classic musical comedy, with occasional original productions.

Centre in Vancouver for Performing Arts

777 Homer St. 604-602-0616. www.centreinvancouver.com.

Once known as the Ford Centre, this striking building across from Library Square was designed by renowned architect Moshe Safdie. The conical glass tower over the entrance is one of those love-it-or-hate-it designs that modern architecture

---

Tickets Tonight

Tickets for many musical and theatre performances can be had for half-price on the day of the show at Tickets Tonight, in the main Tourism Vancouver Visitor Infocentre *(200 Burrard St.; 604-684-2787; www.ticketstonight.ca)*.

The **Alliance for Arts & Culture** is a clearinghouse for performance arts of all kinds in Vancouver, and maintains a comprehensive schedule of events at their office at 938 Howe Street *(604-681-3535; www.allianceforarts.com)*.

seems to relish. Recently reopened after a six-year hiatus, the Centre is Vancouver's venue for touring Broadway musicals such as *42nd Street* and *Fosse*.

Queen Elizabeth Theatre

Hamilton & Dunsmuir Sts. 604-665-3050. www.city.vancouver.bc.ca/theatres.

Home to the city's opera company as well as its principal ballet troupe, this 2,800-seat theatre boasts a 70ft-wide proscenium arch stage. **Vancouver Opera Company** *(604-683-0222; www.vanopera.bc.ca)* offers four or five productions a year here ranging from standards—

Mozart, Puccini, Verdi—to original productions that tend toward the avant-garde. People still talk about a notorious production of Strauss' *Salome*, in the mid-1990s, that was directed by Canadian filmmaker Atom Egoyan. **Ballet British Columbia** also struts their stuff at the "Queen-E," as it's called *(604-732-5003; www.balletbc.com)*. The 1959 theatre is currently planning a redesign to improve its acoustics and sight lines.

Stanley Theatre

2750 Granville St. 604-687-5315. www.artsclub.com.

A massive community fund-raising project enabled the Arts Club Theatre company to take over this historic Art Deco building in 1998. Restored to their 1930s grandeur, the theater's friezes, sconces and chandeliers glisten anew. Productions here tend to be revues, musicals and classic Broadway plays.

Vancouver Playhouse

Hamilton St. at Dunsmuir St. 604-873-3311. www.vancouverplayhouse.com.

Vancouver's leading repertory theatre company offers a half-dozen productions a year of mainstream and avant-garde dramas, ranging from works by Anton Chekhov to David Mamet. Resident actors are joined by national and international stars for a typical three-week run.

Vancouver Symphony

884 Granville St. 604-876-3434. www.vancouversymphony.ca.

While it regularly presents classic works by Beethoven, Brahms, Tchaikovsky and Mahler, the Vancouver Symphony frequently performs and occasionally commissions works by Western Canada composers during its year-long season; these pieces often incorporate elements of First Nations music. Local musicians are featured, too, including members of the prodigal Parker clan, whose three sons are all established pianists. The symphony shares the Orpheum Theatre *(see p 68)* with other local and national touring companies.

More Musts for Performing Arts

Chan Centre for the Performing Arts – *6265 Crescent Rd., University of British Columbia campus. 604-822-9197. www.chancentre.com.* This sparkling facility at UBC is an elegant mid-size performance hall that welcomes national stars to its three stages.

Dal Richards Orchestra – *604-681-6060. www.dalrichards.com.* Western Canada's leading practitioners of big band and swing music make regular appearances throughout the Lower Mainland.

The Dance Centre – *604-606-6400. www.thedancecentre.ca.* Vancouver is a hotbed for modern and ethnic dance—especially Chinese and Japanese—and this clearinghouse organization maintains a schedule of performances at various venues.

Firehall Arts Centre – *280 E. Cordova St. 604-689-0926. www.firehall-artscentre.ca.* Firehall hosts avant-garde drama and performance art, both local and touring, on the east side of downtown.

Vancouver East Cultural Centre – *1895 Venables St. 604-251-1363. www.vecc.bc.ca.* Live music and theatre hold the stage at this unusual historic venue, the renovated 1909 Grandview Methodist Church.

Vancouver TheatreSports League – *1601 Johnston St., Granville Island. 604-738-7013. www.vtsl.com.* This legendary troupe concentrates on impromptu comedy and audience-participation events—an astounding 260 performances a year.

Starry, Starry Nights

Two outdoor venues offer theatre performances under the summer skies in Vancouver, both in city parks:

- **Theatre Under the Stars** takes place in Stanley Park's Malkin Bowl, a 1,200-seat amphitheatre set in a fir and cedar forest near the Vancouver Aquarium. Performances of repertory plays, usually musicals, take place from mid-July through August *(604-687-0174; www.tuts.bc.ca)*.
- **Bard on the Beach** is a summer-long Shakespeare festival staged in Vanier Park, near the start of False Creek, *(take Burrard St. Bridge south and turn right on Chestnut St.)*. Elizabethan-style tents, and musical and juggling acts contribute to the festival atmosphere. The city skyline and North Shore Mountains provide the backdrop for the open stage. Three or four Shakespeare plays rotate during the seasonal schedule *(Jun–Sept; 604-739-0559 or 877-739-0559; www.bardonthebeach.com)*.

Festive Indeed

If you like festivals, you've come to the right place. Vancouver shows its dedication to the arts through a stellar, year-long lineup of festivals devoted to performance and cultural arts. Check the alternative weekly newpaper *Georgia Straight (www.straight.com)* to see what's happening when you're in town.

Festival Vancouver

Various locations. 604-688-1152. www.festivalvancouver.bc.ca. Music of every description, from chamber to jazz, rings in 50 concerts during this citywide fest in early August.

HSBC Celebration of Light

English Bay. 604-641-1193. www.celebration-of-light.com. What's unique about Vancouver's annual four-night showcase *(late Jul–early Aug)* is that the fireworks shower over English Bay to intensify the visual experience. The display is keyed to music, and fireworks artists from three countries compete against each other for first prize. It's free, too; the best seats are along English Bay Beach (the *very* best seats are at the reserved-seating barbecue at English Bay Bathhouse), but the show is visible from Kitsilano and the lower end of False Creek as well. If you want to be up close, arrive in late afternoon—thousands of people jockey for position.

Vancouver Folk Music Festival

Jericho Beach. 604-602-9798. www.thefestival.bc.ca. Folk artists from around North America bring dozens of different music styles, from Tejano to French-Canadian, to Jericho Beach in mid-July.

Vancouver Fringe Festival

Various locations. 604-257-0350. www.vancouverfringe.com. Fringe is perfect for a city whose political and cultural climate is Canada's most progressive. At this two-week festival in mid-September, you'll see performance art, impromptu groups, radical drama and multimedia presentations.

Vancouver International Comedy Festival

Granville Island. 604-683-0883. www.comedyfest.com. Jokes about rain are a mainstay at this event, even though it's held during the driest part of the year at the end of July.

Vancouver International Film Festival

Various locations. 604-685-0260. www.viff.org. The stars all come out between late September and mid-October for this annual affair. Though it focuses somewhat on Canadian cinema, 300 films from 50 countries are included.

Vancouver International Jazz Festival

Various locations. 604-872-5200. www.coastaljazz.ca. One of the major such gatherings in North America, this annual two-week affair at the end of June draws stars from around the world. More than a dozen venues participate, from intimate nightclubs to mid-size performance halls. Don't miss the two-day street festival in Gastown and Yaletown.

Must Shop

Vancouver's remarkable cultural diversity—with its European, Asian and Native heritages—makes shopping here a treat. In Vancouver you'll find items not available in most other North American cities, including traditional First Nations mask art and nontraditional chocolate truffles shaped to look like First Nations art. Asian foodstuffs and furnishings in Chinatown complement European antiques along Main Street. Of course, many American visitors flock to the city's cigar stores to buy Cuban smokes forbidden in the States.

Robson Street★★

Once known as "Robsonstrasse" to reflect the street's erstwhile German character, this thoroughfare leading from downtown to the West End has transformed itself into a cosmopolitan district with ethnic flair. It is particularly popular with Asian teens, whose main objective for flying across the Pacific is to stroll Robson. (Yes, really.)

On the blocks of Robson between Hornby and Denman streets, you can wear out your wallet buying everything from high fashion to yoga togs. When you're ready for a break, Robson is a prime place to people-watch. Grab a seat at an outdoor cafe and check out the leather-clad bikers sipping lattés at Starbucks; purple-haired counterculture advocates heading for a demonstration at the Vancouver Art Gallery; Japanese schoolgirls walking hand-in-hand from boutique to boutique; and smartly clad office workers scurrying back from lunch. It's a parade you won't soon forget.

Robson Street Shopping Lineup

La Casa del Habano *(no. 980; 604-609-0511; www.havanahouse.com)* offers a wide, if pricey, selection of Cuban cigars.

Lush *(no. 1020; 604-687-5874; www.lushcanada.com)* is a British soap and cosmetics maker whose delectable aroma drifts out onto the street.

La Vie en Rose *(no. 1009; 604-684-5600; www.lavieenrose.ca)* purveys the very finest European lingerie.

Roots Canada *(no. 1001; 604-683-4305; www.roots.com)* is a branch of the clothing company that achieved world renown with its popularity at the Salt Lake Winter Olympics in 2002.

Oh Yes Vancouver *(no. 1167; 604-687-3187)* is a shopping rarity, a souvenir store that sells items actually worth taking home.

Granville Island Public Market★ *– Granville Island. See Musts for Fun.*

Antique Row

South Main St., between Broadway & 12th Ave.

The usual selection of furniture, crockery and jewellery is here, with a tilt toward British colonial leftovers. The **Blue Heron**, at no. 3516, is a great resource for antiquers—its stock in trade is books on antiques *(604-874-8401)*.

The Bay

674 Granville St. 604-681-6211. www.hbc.com.

Yes, this is the corporate descendant of the Hudson's Bay Company whose traders established most of the first European outposts in Canada. Housed in a massive Beaux-Arts building downtown, the Bay has morphed into a mainstream department store. But you can still get Hudson's Bay blankets, just as trappers and traders did 150 years ago—you'd have trouble bartering for them with beaver skins, though.

Dorothy Grant

1656 W. 75th Ave. 604 681 0201. www.dorothygrant.com.

Haida artist Dorothy Grant superimposes traditional First Nations designs in vivid colours on fine, ultra-chic wool and microfiber clothing. Her pricey coats, shawls and dress jackets will make a lifetime addition to anyone's closet.

Lonsdale Quay

On the North Shore of Burrard Inlet. 604-985-6261. www.lonsdalequay.com. Open year-round daily 9:30am–6:30pm (Fri until 9pm; restaurants open later).

Aside from the array of farm-fresh produce and 90 shops and cafes that await shoppers here, the best part about Lonsdale Quay is getting there. Take the Seabus ferry, which docks right at the quay and provides dandy views of the North Shore Mountains and downtown Vancouver en route.

Sinclair Centre

757 W. Hastings St., at Granville St. 604 659 1009. www.sinclaircentre.com. See Landmarks.

Four historic buildings downtown are now linked under one glass roof as a sparkling retail complex with designer boutiques galore.

Neighbourhoods for Shopping

Chinatown★★ – *Bounded by Keefer, Abbott, Hastings & Gore Sts. See Neighbourhoods.*

Gastown★ – *Water Street between Carrall & Richard Sts. See Historic Sites.*

Though Gastown itself is the home of an extensive array of T-shirt and tacky souvenir shops, chiefly along Water Street (how many little cans of maple syrup from Quebec does anyone need?), the adjoining streets have some more interesting retail outlets. Westernwear stores, curio outlets, home furnishings, and economical Native artwork are among the offerings.

Gastown Standouts: Sikora's Classical Records *(432 West Hastings St.; 604-685-0625; www.sikorasclassical.com)* is a treasure trove for anyone who likes classical and world music—that's all there is—with more than 10,000 titles. At **McLeod's Books** *(455 W. Pender St; 604-681-7654; www.abebooks. com/home/macleods)* tables and shelves are piled high with used volumes spanning an array of subjects and authors far beyond the ken of modern chain outlets.

Yaletown★ – *Bounded by Davie, Homer, Nelson & Cambie Sts., and Pacific Blvd. See Neighbourhoods.*

Broadway District – *Broadway & 4th Ave., roughly from Oak St. west to Arbutus St.* Vancouver's most extensive retail area is a mile-long stretch of Broadway and Fourth Avenue, south of False Creek. The district is chockablock with hundreds of stores, cafes and galleries, virtually all of which are independent; many concentrate on locally made or Canadian goods, and the atmosphere is distinctively welcoming.

At **International Travel Maps and Books** *(530 W. Broadway; 604-879-3621; www.itmb.com)* adventure traveller Jack Joyce carries hundreds of his company's own titles, along with a host of others. Check out **Chocolate Arts** *(2037 W. 4th Ave.; 604-739-0475; www.chocolatearts.com),* where beautifully shaped confections bear First Nations designs—eagles, orcas, ravens—and pose an existential dilemma: enjoying the chocolate destroys the art.

Denman Street – *West End. See Neighbourhoods.*

Gear for the Great Outdoors

The east end of the Broadway district is fast becoming a mecca for all manner of outdoor and recreational supplies. **Mountain Equipment Co-op** *(130 W. Broadway; 604-872-7858; www.mec.ca)*, a home-grown Vancouver institution that resembles its American counterpart REI, carries high-quality sporting gear of every description. Store personnel here also have a priceless inventory of information; ask them if you want to know something about outdoor recreation in Western Canada. On the other side of the street, **Altus Mountain Gear** has whatever you need for an Everest expedition *(137 W. Broadway; 604-876-5255)*.

First Nations Art

Masks, carvings, wood panels and bentwood boxes made by Western Canada's First Nations artisans are among the world's most distinctive artworks, instantly recognisable and immensely valuable. Any collector would treasure a cedar panel with vividly etched and brightly coloured illustrations of the whales, bears, eagles and ravens that are significant spirits to BC's coastal peoples. Especially hard to find (and hard to make) are bentwood boxes, in which the cedar panels are formed into four sides, usually adorned with discreet decorative designs.

Native art is the subject of some controversy, though not all is made by First Nations people; and not all is even very good. If you care about the authenticity of a piece, your best bet is to buy at a top-quality, reputable dealer—and expect to pay top dollar. Of course, what you get is the equal, in aesthetic and financial value, of any fine European or American painting. The best Inuit soapstone sculptures and Northwest Coast masks and wall panels can cost many thousands of dollars.

Best Outlets for First Nations Art:

Marion Scott Gallery *(308 Water St., Gastown; 604-685-1934; www.marion-scottgallery.com)* has an especially fine selection of Inuit stone and ivory carvings.

Spirit Wrestler Gallery *(47 Water St.; Gastown; 604-669-8813; www.spirit-wrestler.com)* specializes in Inuit carving and Northwest Coast masks.

Hill's Native Art *(165 Water St., Gastown; 604-685-4249; www.hillsnativeart.com)* is the most reputable dealer for less expensive First Nations art.

Eagle Spirit Gallery *(1803 Maritime Mews, Granville Island; 604-801-5205; www.eaglespiritgallery.com)* features superlative Northwest Coast masks and totems, all splendidly displayed.

Must Not Take Home

One of the great attractions of Vancouver shopping—for some Americans, at least—is that Cuban rum and cigars are freely available. US customs officials at Vancouver airports and the border are ever on the watch for these items. But it's perfectly legal to puff away on an Uppmann cigar or imbibe Havana Club rum in Canada. Just make sure you dispose of contents, bottles and wrappers before you leave the country.

Though Vancouver is a film- and music-industry capital, raves and disco just don't cut it here. Search out Vancouver's nightlife in the low-key lounges of the city's major hotels, and in myriad small restaurant/nightclubs, where you can see live performers. For the complete scoop on Vancouver nightlife, pick up a free copy of the alternative weekly newspaper, *Georgia Straight*, or check the Thursday entertainment section of the *Vancouver Sun*.

Bacchus Lounge

845 Hornby St., in the Wedgewood Hotel, Downtown. 604-608-5319. www.wedgewoodhotel.com/hotel/bacchus.html.

When you see the languorous painting of Bacchus that hangs over the piano in this elegant nightspot, you'll know their philosophy: Indulge yourself, peacefully. Jazz singers ply the keyboards here most nights of the week. The relaxed setting encourages conversation, and the adjacent, fully enclosed cigar lounge draws athletes and celebrities.

Gerard Lounge

845 Burrard St., in the Sutton Place Hotel, Downtown. 604-682-5511. www.vancouver.suttonplace.com.

This nightspot's clubby, quiet ambience is legendary for attracting film celebrities—and you can indeed spot stars here. Its low-key atmosphere also makes the lounge a comfortable space to sit and talk.

Irish Heather

217 Carrall St., Gastown. 604-688-9779. www.irishheather.com.

This club is a great place to hear one of Vancouver's most popular genres—Celtic music. Irish Heather features live performers most nights, including occasional appearances by well-known local bands.

900 West Lounge

900 W. Georgia St., in the Hotel Vancouver, Downtown. 604-669-9378. www.fairmont.com/hotelvancouver.

Downtown's largest adult lounge encompasses a vast open space in the Art Moderne lobby of the venerable Hotel Vancouver. Piano/vocal performers entertain nightly, and hors-d'oeuvres are available from the hotel restaurant.

O'Doul's

1300 Robson St., in the Listel Vancouver Hotel, West End. 604-661-1400. www.odoulsrestaurant.com.

This chophouse restaurant morphs into downtown's leading emporium for jazzy torch singing on weekend nights. The single-malt scotch selection is especially good.

Railway Club

579 Dunsmuir St., Downtown. 604-681-1625. www.therailwayclub.com.

Lines are often long to get into this live-rock and alternative-music emporium. And if you aren't dressed right (don't show up in your rodeo duds or three-piece suit), you might as well go someplace else.

Richard's on Richards

1036 Richards St., Downtown. 604-687-6794. www.richardsonrichards.com.

Vancouver's most conspicuous dance club offers DJ music every night, on a rotating schedule of styles, from hip-hop to electronica, with live bands on weekends, and periodic hip-hop comedy nights.

Yale Hotel

1300 Granville St., Yaletown. 604-681-9253. www.theyale.ca.

Blues, with both Canadian and American bands, is the theme here. The stage in this Victorian-era building has hosted international stars such as Bonnie Raitt, Buddy Guy and Elvin Bishop.

Yaletown Brewing Co.

1111 Mainland St., Yaletown. 604-681-2739. www.drinkfreshbeer.com.

Yaletown's leading sports bar is a boisterous place to be on hockey night, and before and after games at BC Place and GM Place. Pub-style food here is supplemented by house-made ales, stouts and other hearty brews.

Gay Nightlife

Vancouver has one of the leading gay communities in Canada, and the gay and lesbian entertainment scene is dynamic.

Celebrities Night Club – *1022 Davie St., Downtown. 604-681-6180. www.celebritiesnightclub.com.* Newly renovated, with state-of-the art sound, this club offers a weekly line-up and two floors for dancing and bars.

Lotus Club – *455 Abbott St., Downtown. 604-685-7777.* Downstairs at the Lotus is a lively venue for DJ dance music.

The Odyssey – *1251 Howe St., Downtown. 604-689-5256. www.theodysseynightclub.com.* One of Vancouver's hottest nightclubs, the Odyssey draws both straights and gays for drag shows and film screenings.

The Oasis Pub – *1240 Thurlow St., West End. 604-685-1724. www.theoasispub.com.* Customers here enjoy a huge selection of tapas and martinis, accompanied by piano music.

When the Stars Come Out

With an average of a half-dozen film productions underway at any given time in Vancouver, star-gazing is a popular pastime. The best places for seeing stars are the Gerard Lounge in the Sutton Place Hotel and the cigar room at Bacchus Lounge, in the Wedgewood Hotel. Celebs tend to favour Gotham Steakhouse downtown *(615 Seymour St.; 604-605-8282; www.gothamsteakhouse.com)*; Joe Fortes Seafood & Chop House in the West End *(777 Thurlow St.; see Must Eat)*; and Yaletown's Elbow Room Cafe *(560 Davie St.; 604-685-3628; www.theelbowroomcafe.com)* for a late breakfast.

Yes, it does occasionally rain in Vancouver (more than 150 days a year report some sort of precipitation), but don't wait for a rainy day to luxuriate in one of the city's elegant spas. Most major spas in Vancouver are associated with upscale hotels, but even if you're not a guest at a particular property, you can still take advantage of its spa. Reservations are a good idea, but if your spa experience is a last-minute choice, many of the ones listed below can usually fit you in for a treatment.

Absolute Spa at the Century

1015 Burrard St., at the Century Plaza Hotel. 604-684-2772. www.absolutespa.com.

Located in the lower level of the Century Plaza Hotel in mid-downtown, the Absolute pioneered the spa industry in Vancouver. Its fine reputation and established clientele combine to make it hard to get into at the last minute. If you do get in, you'll find a full menu of pampering here, from facials and manicures to mud wraps—in addition to such complementary services as light meals, eucalyptus steam, and an ozone-treated pool. Got jet lag? Absolute has three branch operations at Vancouver International Airport (two in the terminals and one at the Fairmont Vancouver Airport Hotel).

Vida Wellness Spa, The Sutton Place Hotel Vancouver

845 Burrard St., at the Sutton Place Hotel. 604-642-2999. www.suttonplace.com.

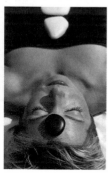

Yes, those Hollywood types do like to pamper themselves. Vida Wellness Spa, whose host hotel, Sutton Place, is a huge favourite with the film industry, has long experience in taking care of discriminating spa clientele who demand the most gratifying, most comprehensive and most effective body treatments. Accordingly, the spa's stone massage utilizes 54 hot stones and 18 cool ones to both relax and re-energize your muscles. Treat yourself to the ultimate package, which combines a massage, facial, manicure, pedicure, reflexology and—ah, Hollywood—winds up with a champagne lunch.

The Spa at The Fairmont Hotel Vancouver

900 W. Georgia St. 604-648-2909. www.fairmont.com.

The Fairmont's spa treatments include wraps, facials and infusions using Canadian rose-hip oil, whose healing properties are substantial. Try one of the European kur treatments, which replenish your body's lost nutrients using thermal mineral water, sea salts from France, mineral-rich moor mud and purifying algae. If you want to work up a sweat before your massage, the facility includes fitness equipment along with saunas, a whirlpool, and swimming pools for adults and children.

The Spa at the Wedgewood Hotel

845 Hornby St., at the Wedgewood Hotel. 604-608-5340. www.wedgewoodhotel.com.

Vancouver's best-known boutique hotel has added a spa that draws on the hotel's international flavour for its character. The all-natural Epicuren line of skin products, used in facials, scrubs and other treatments, is designed to stimulate the body's immune system. Other distinctive treatments include Lavender Body Bliss, a scrub, wrap and lotion application all using lavender essence.

Skoah

1011 Hamilton St. 604-642-0200. www.skoah.com.

The focus in this hip Yaletown spa is on skin care for the head and back. Try "sunny side down," a facial for your back with cleansing, exfoliation, detoxification and massage. The "up and down" combines facials for both head and back. Treatments here are more reasonably priced than at the big hotel spas.

Vida Wellness Spa,
The Sheraton Vancouver Wall Centre Hotel

1088 Burrard St., at the Sheraton Wall Centre. 604-682-8410. www.vidawellness.com.

Located in downtown Vancouver's largest hotel, Vida specializes in applying Ayurveda, the ancient Indian herbal wellness regime, to modern practices and techniques. Body scrubs, wraps and massages utilizing Ayurvedic essences and lotions all induce a heightened sense of health and balance.

Destination Spas

These two spa getaways blend Canada's Western ranching tradition with wholly modern health and wellness philosophies. BC's cattle-ranching district, the Cariboo, is four to five hours by car from Vancouver.

Echo Valley Ranch

On Jesmond Rd., in Clinton. 404km/251mi north of Vancouver. 250-459-2386 or 800-253-8831. www.evranch.com. 20 rooms.

A New Age retreat overlooking Fraser Canyon, this ranch ranks as a North American centre for the teaching and practice of Thai massage. A day of riding, a pampering massage and the lodge's Austrian-inspired cuisine induce a sense of serenity as you watch the sun set over the Chilcotin Mountains.

The Hills Health Ranch

On Hwy. 97 in the town of 108-Mile Ranch. 487km/302mi north of Vancouver. 250-791-5225. www.spabc.com. 46 units.

This health retreat/guest ranch draws clients from all over North America, who come for intensive rejuvenation programs combining exercise, recreation in the Cariboo parkland, body treatments and healthy cuisine. The ranch's signature rose-hip oil, made from rose hips gathered each fall in the area, is a superlative therapeutic lotion.

If you can tear yourself away from Vancouver, it's worth a sojourn to the **Lower Mainland.** In this area, which stretches from the Strait of Georgia east to Hope and the Cascade Range, bounded on the south by the US border, and on the north by the southern flanks of the towering Coast Mountains, you'll find everything from small, U-pick berry farms to spectacular canyons cutting through the mountains.

Home to some two million people, the Lower Mainland includes the Fraser River Delta, the lower Fraser Valley, and the foothills of both the Coast and Cascade ranges. Though it makes up just two percent of British Columbia's land mass, this region contains half the population of the entire province. Burgeoning urban growth is a reality these days, but a lot of this land remains pastoral, relying on good soil and mild weather for its agricultural bounty. Much of Canada's fresh produce is grown in the region, including BC's well-known hothouse tomatoes and cucumbers.

North and West Vancouver

These two communities were developed as suburbs of Vancouver, but have long since established their own identities, with small city centres, their own

Bridging the Gap

The **Lions Gate Bridge** *(see Landmarks),* which joins North and West Vancouver to Vancouver proper via the Stanley Park Causeway, is just three lanes wide. It backs up considerably during the morning and evening commute. Though visitors are usually travelling the opposite direction, counter-commute traffic has only one lane on the bridge, so the trip may be no faster. Allow an extra 20 minutes if you are crossing during morning or evening rush hour.

parks, schools and governments. Residents are fond of pointing out that in one direction they have quick access to one of the great cosmopolitan cities of North America—and in the other, heading up into the North Shore Mountains, they have access to the beginning of one of the biggest, wildest and most spectacular wilderness areas on the continent. The modern, cliff-hugging, multimillion-dollar mansions that line the shore westward from West Vancouver's downtown represent the most valuable real estate in Canada.

Lighthouse Park★★

Off Marine Dr., 8km/5mi northwest of downtown via Lions Gate Bridge; follow Marine Dr. west to Beacon Lane. 604-925-7200. www.westvancouver.ca. Open year-round daily 6:30am–10:30pm.

This protected enclave on Point Atkinson at the westernmost end of West Vancouver has three wonderful facets: the Lower Mainland's largest remaining old growth forest, inviting hiking trails that lead through the woods down to the shore, and memorable **views★★★** of Vancouver from the shoreline's rocky headlands. The park's untouched woods have made it a popular location for film crews, for whom it has stood in for forests around the world. For anyone, it is the best place in the Vancouver area to see old-growth trees.

Old-growth Forest – Fortunately, the temperate rain forest that now forms part of the park was not logged during Vancouver's development. Today, the big trees (some up to 500 years old, with diameters approaching 2m/7ft) anchor a classic old-growth ecosystem. Huckleberries, vine maples, scrub oak and red-barked madronas (called arbutus in Canada) fill open spaces where light filters through the conifer canopy overhead.

Hiking in Lighthouse Park – Walking the park's paths, in the serene, light-dappled forest understory, hints at what the entire Lower Mainland was like before European settlement. The best path through the forest parallels the road on the west side of the peninsula *(follow signs to the outdoor theatre)*. Once you reach the **Point Atkinson Lighthouse** complex, shoreline trails lead both east and west along the rocky headlands.

Tree-mendous

Douglas fir isn't really a fir. Western red cedar isn't a true cedar, either. And western hemlock doesn't have anything to do with what Socrates drank. Misidentification and accidents of history have created great confusion over the names of the most prominent forest trees of the Pacific Coast—but there's no confusion over their size, beauty and ecological significance.

Douglas firs are usually the biggest, most massive trees with thick, reddish-brown corrugated bark that withstands fire well. They can grow to 91.5m/300ft in height and 3m/10ft in diameter. Red cedars have fabric-like bark, drooping branches and foliage, sturdy flared bases; they favour wetter locations. Western hemlocks have smoother, thinner bark, and lacier foliage than Douglas firs, but approach similar size and age. A true, mature temperate rain forest, like the one in Lighthouse Park, has a mix of all three types, in various sizes and ages.

Sea to Sky Highway★★

Rte. 99 runs 102km/63mi from Horseshoe Bay in West Vancouver north to Whistler.
Visitor information: 604-892-9244 or www.britishcolumbia.com.
Sights below are organized from south to north.

Even if you don't want to follow Route 99 all the way to Whistler, be sure to drive along at least a part of this highway for incredible **views★★★** of the blue-green waters of the **Howe Sound** with mountains all around it. Extending some 48km/30mi into the Coast Mountains, this deep fjord provides some of the province's most dramatic coastal scenery between the picturesque ferry port of Horseshoe Bay and the town of Squamish to the north.

BC Museum of Mining★★ – *38km/24mi north of Horseshoe Bay on Rte. 99, in Britannia Beach. 604-896-2233. Open early May–mid-Oct daily 9am–4:30pm. Rest of the year Mon–Fri 9am–4:30pm. $14.98 ($6 in winter). www.bcmuseumofmining.org.*

This former copper mine enjoyed its heyday beginning in World War I, when Britain and her allies relied on its output. By 1929 it was the largest copper mine in the British Empire. Closed in 1974, the mine now welcomes visitors who pile into ore cars for a trip into the 671m/2,200ft **supply shaft.** The eerie eight-level **concentrator building** has often served as a film set.

Xá:ytem Interpretive Centre

In the early 1990s, stone tools found during preliminary work for a subdivision near Mission led to the discovery of the remains of an extensive settlement and spiritual site of the Sto:lo people, who lived along the shores of the Fraser River long before Europeans arrived. Today, in the cedar longhouse of the **Xá:ytem Interpretive Centre** *(35087 Lougheed Hwy., Mission; open Jul–Aug daily 9am–4:30pm; rest of year Mon–Sat 9am–4:30pm; $10; 604-820-9725; www.xaytem.ca)* you can learn how the Sto:lo people flourished in this area. The Centre also offers hands-on workshops where you can use traditional methods to create your own cedar basket, mat or drum.

Shannon Falls★ – *45km/28mi north of Horseshoe Bay.* A short hike from the site's parking lot along Route 99 leads to a viewing point at the base of these impressive falls, which cascade 335m/1,100ft over a cliff here.

West Coast Railway Heritage Park★ – *1km/.6mi west of Rte. 99 on Government Rd. in Squamish. 604-898-9336. www.wcra.org/heritage. Open year-round daily 10am–5pm. $10.* Western Canada's trains are the stars here, especially the painstakingly restored 1890 **British Columbia★★**, a Canadian Pacific business car decked out with inlaid mahogany and leather. Spend some time roaming the grounds to see the myriad other cars and engines that fill the yards.

Whistler★★ – *See Excursions.*

Capilano Canyon★

From Lions Gate Bridge, take Marine Dr. east to Capilano Rd., Exit 14, in North Vancouver. The suspension bridge entrance is at 3735 Capilano Rd. 604-985-7474. www.capbridge.com. Open May–Sept daily 8:30am–8pm. Rest of the year daily 9am–dusk. Closed Dec 25. $26.95.

You'll appreciate this deep canyon best by taking the narrow pedestrian **Capilano Suspension Bridge** 70m/230ft above the Capilano River. This wire-rope bridge, one of the best-known in North America, sways and bounces to the thrill of visitors as they walk across it. The entrance complex is a hodge-podge of knick-knack shops, cafes and exhibits ranging from cigar-store Indians to a history of logging in the area.

Cypress Provincial Park★

12km/7mi northwest of downtown Vancouver via Lions Gate Bridge & Hwy. 1 to Cypress Mountain Rd. 604-926-5612. www.env.gov.bc.ca/bcparks. Open year-round daily. $5 parking.

Clinging to the heights of the Coast Range above West Vancouver, this ski and snow sports area will be the site of the snowboard and freestyle events during the 2010 Winter Olympics. In summer, hiking trails lead through the western red-cedar and yellow-cedar forests for which the park is named.

Get Out on the Rivers

Native people and early settlers relied on rivers to get around, but today most people just cross over them or catch fleeting glimpses from their cars. **Sasquatch Tours** *(604-796-1221; www.sasquatchtours.com)* provides a fascinating native perspective of bald eagles, native rock paintings and salmon spawning grounds as they take you down the Harrison River from the docks at Harrison Hot Springs. **Fraser River Safari** *(7057 Mershon St., Mission; 604-826-7361; www.FraserRiverSafari.com)* navigates the busy Fraser River in its enclosed jet boat through ever-changing shallow gravel bars to the confluence of the clear waters of the Harrison River with the turbulent Fraser.

Grouse Mountain★

From Lions Gate Bridge, take Capilano Rd. to 6400 Nancy Greene Way, North Vancouver. 604-984-0661. www.grousemountain.com. Gondola open year-round daily 9am–10pm; closed Dec 24–25; $29.95.

The steep gondola ride from the base of this attraction carries passengers almost 914m/3,000ft up to a ridgeline recreation complex that offers unmatched **views★★** of the Vancouver area. Skiing and snow sports are popular in winter, and hiking and biking rule in summer. Go simply to experience the ride and the view from the top (both are well worth the time and money), and enjoy a meal on the outdoor patio of the mountaintop restaurant *(call for reservations),* a peerless place to have lunch or dinner on a clear summer day.

Lynn Canyon Park★

17km/10.5mi north of Vancouver via Lions Gate Bridge. Take Hwy. 1 to Lynn Valley Rd. exit; turn right on Lynn Valley Rd. and right on Peters Rd. to the park. 604-981-3103. www.dnv.org/ecology. Open year-round daily 7am; closing hours vary.

This 249.5ha/617-acre regional preserve straddles the canyon of a swift and cold North Shore river, the Lynn. Trails lead along the canyon rim, through deep forest and into the gorge, where emerald swimming holes await hardy souls. A short **suspension bridge★** carries a trail across the canyon. Exercise caution when near the cliff edges and when swimming in the river.

Capilano River Regional Park

Access from Capilano Rd., just north of the Capilano suspension bridge; and at Cleveland Dam, north end of Capilano Rd. 604-224-5739. www.gvrd.bc.ca.

Encompassing the river's narrow gorge and its hillsides, this park has peaceful hiking trails, streamside spots for picnicking and contemplation, and scattered patches of old-growth forest. The lower entrance to the park leads to the **Capilano Salmon Hatchery,** where visitors can take a self-guided tour to learn about the life-cycle of migrating salmon and steelhead. At the north end of the park, **Cleveland Dam** impounds a drinking-water reservoir; the top of the dam has excellent views of the Lions, the two peaks for which Lions Gate is named.

Indian Arm

For a different type of beach experience, try Indian Arm, the southernmost fjord in North America. This long tongue of saltwater stretches from the east end of Burrard Inlet northward into the heart of the Coast Range. Indian Arm quickly passes from its urban beginnings into wilderness, with snowcapped peaks above, waterfalls rushing over stone faces, and sandy coves where emerald waters are just warm enough for the adventurous to take a dip. Both canoeing and kayaking are possible in this protected inlet; **Deep Cove Canoe & Kayak Centre** *(2156 Banbury Rd., North Vancouver; 604-929-2268; www.deepcovekayak.com)* offers rentals and guided tours.

East Fraser Valley

The narrow, 145km/90mi expanse of flat river bottom stretching south and east from Vancouver has long been the city's agricultural fringe—and now is its suburban growth area as well. The municipalities of Richmond, Burnaby, Delta, Surrey and New Westminster all have their own city centres, and their own attractions. But they are inarguably satellites to Vancouver, which connects to them via the two Lower Mainland freeways, Highway 99 south to the US border, and Highway 1 (the Trans-Canada Highway) east to Hope.

East of Surrey, development lessens, and the countryside reverts to farmland between Langley and Abbotsford, and on to Chilliwack. The latter community is famed for its produce stands, which in August and September offer huge bins of fresh-picked Chilliwack corn.

Burnaby Village Museum★

14km/9mi east of Vancouver via Hastings St. E. east to Hwy. 1; take the Kensington Ave. exit and go south on Kensington Ave.; turn left on Canada Way. 6501 Deer Lake Ave., in Deer Lake Park, Burnaby. 604-293-6501. www.burnaby.ca. Open May–Sept daily 11am–4:30pm, late Nov–Jan 2 daily noon–5:30pm. $7.75.

Cotton candy spins at a picture show, penny candy fills jars at the general store. The clank of a hammer on hot iron resounds from the blacksmith. There's a moving picture show, an apothecary and an ice-cream parlour. This is life in the Lower Mainland circa the turn of the 19th century. Most of the 30 restored buildings in the extensive complex were moved here from elsewhere. Costumed interpreters here offer insights on daily life of a bygone era. The 1912 **carousel★** delights kids now as much as it did nearly a century ago.

Fort Langley National Historic Site★

56km/35mi southeast of Vancouver via Hwy. 1. Glover St. & Mavis Ave., in Langley. 604-513-4777. www.pc.gc.ca/lhn-nhs/bc/langley. Open daily 10am–5pm (to 4pm Nov–mid-Mar). $7.15.

Opened as a Hudson's Bay Company trading post in 1827, this fort played a key role in the settlement of British Columbia for 50 years. Trappers and traders were the first to pass through; then, starting in 1860, gold rushers came here on their way to the Cariboo. BC was declared a British crown colony at the post's **Big House** in 1858—an event still commemorated here today. Set on a cottonwood-shaded rise beside the Fraser River, the compound includes restored or reconstructed buildings; costumed interpreters play the part of carpenters, trappers, schoolmarms, coopers (barrel-makers) and blacksmiths.

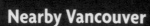

Harrison Hot Springs★

129km/80mi east of Vancouver. Take Hwy. 1 on the south side of the Fraser River to the exit for Agassiz-Harrison (Exit 135) beyond Chilliwack; then Rte. 9 across the river to Kent and continue north on Rte. 9 for 6km/4mi.

This famed resort remains the nearest hot spring to Vancouver and a strong draw for weekend getaways. Set on the south end of Harrison Lake (the springs were discovered by boaters who noticed an upwelling of unusually warm water), the resort offers broad sandy beaches that are the site of a celebrated sandcastle competition each September. At **Harrison Hot Springs Resort and Spa** *(100 Esplanade; 604-796-2244; www.harrisonresort.com)*, you'll find lodging, dining, spa treatments and assorted bathing pools.

Hell's Gate Airtram★

52km/32mi north of Hope via Hwy. 1. 604-867-9277. www.hellsgateairtram.com. Open mid-April–mid-October daily. $15.

Early explorer Simon Fraser named this terrifying narrows along the river that bears his name. He wrote in his journal: "We had to travel where no human being should venture— for surely we have encountered the gates of Hell." Narrowed even farther by late-19C railroad work, this passage is now just 33.5m/110ft wide, and through it roars twice as much water as at Niagara Falls. The airtram's gondola descends 152m/500ft from the highway above and crosses the chasm to a landing on the west side, offering a thrilling ride and great views of the narrows.

Hope★

150km/93mi east of Vancouver via Hwy. 1.

This erstwhile logging centre occupies a small pocket along the Fraser River between the Cascade and Coast mountains, and is considered the farthest reach of the Lower Mainland. (Residents of the rest of interior BC refer to the notorious dichotomy in perspective between themselves and Vancouverites by declaring in jest that they live "beyond Hope.") Chainsaw carving is big in these parts; a guide to the two dozen sculptures scattered about town is available at the **Visitor Infocentre** *(919 Water Ave.; 604-869-2021; www.hopebc.ca).*

Fraser River Delta

At New Westminster, the Fraser River divides into two major arms, forming a classic fan-shaped delta estuary. Although the flatlands of the delta—its fine soils once were home to numerous farms—are now being converted to suburbs, the area's attractions still derive from its fishing and farming history, and its large population of waterfowl and migratory birds.

George C. Reifel Bird Sanctuary★

32km/20mi south of Vancouver via Hwy. 99 (Exit 28) & Hwy. 17. At Ladner, take Ladner Trunk Rd. west to River Rd. and cross the bridge onto Westham Island. Turn right on Robertson Rd. to the sanctuary. 604-946-6980. www.reifelbirdsanctuary.com. Open year-round daily 9am–4pm. $4.

Birders take note: this stopover point on the Pacific flyway is one of the most important bird-watching locales in the Vancouver area—more than 260 species have been sighted. Encompassing 300ha/850 acres of wetlands and marsh in the Fraser River Estuary, the sanctuary lands were set aside in the 1960s by George H. Reifel. During snow goose migration *(Nov and Apr)*, as many as 30,000 of the white geese gather here, creating an unforgettable sight. Don't forget your binoculars.

Steveston Village★

27km/17mi south of Vancouver via Hwy. 99 south to Steveston Hwy. (Exit 32); follow Steveston Hwy. west to Fourth Ave. and turn left. Visitor information: 604-821-5474 or www.steveston.bc.ca.

Salt tang flavours the air. The creak of rigging and hulls on dock lofts along the shore. Mist rolls in off the water. You'll savour the atmosphere of a century-old fishing village in this historic complex. Spurred by the restoration of several of its historic sites, the village itself, with its numerous shops and cafes, has become a destination. Fishing isn't dead here; the marina still berths 1,000 boats, including commercial fishers who ply local waters.

Gulf of Georgia Cannery National Historic Site★ – *12138 Fourth Ave., Steveston Village. 604-664-9009. www.pc.gc.ca/lhn-nhs/bc/georgia. Open Jun–Labour Day daily 10am–5pm, May & Labour Day–mid-Oct Thu–Mon 10am–5pm. $7.15.* The last major cannery on the Fraser River shut down for good in 1979 after almost a century packing salmon, halibut and herring. Now a museum, the complex features a model **canning line** and fascinating exhibits on the heyday of the salmon-packing industry.

The area around Vancouver in British Columbia's southwest corner holds some of the most popular travel destinations in North America. Some, such as Victoria, are urban attractions. Others like Pacific Rim National Park and the Tofino area, rely on their natural wonders to draw visitors. Still others, such as Whistler, combine both: spectacular natural features, outdoor recreation and top-notch civilized amenities. To fully appreciate them all would take months, but a one- or two-day side trip to any of them is eminently worthwhile.

Victoria★★★

On Vancouver Island. Access from Vancouver via ferry only (see Practical Information).

The British colonial flair that has long characterized Victoria is as evident as ever, but savvy travellers look beyond afternoon tea and horse-drawn carriages to enjoy the city's beautiful gardens, multicultural flavour and outstanding natural setting.

Founded in 1843 as a Hudson's Bay Company outpost, and designated the colonial capital in 1862, Victoria was once the next stop on the British Empire circuit after Burma and Hong Kong, from which clipper ships called with tea and other Asian goods. Seat of the provincial government since 1868, Victoria is BC's second-largest metropolitan area, with a population of about 500,000. The mild climate makes it a garden capital and a popular retirement centre as well.

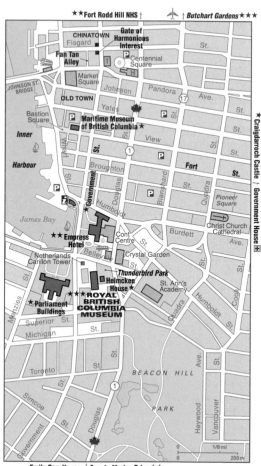

Butchart Gardens★★★

North of Victoria, in Brentwood Bay. Take Hwy. 17 to Keating Cross Rd. 250-652-5256 or 866-652-4422. www.butchartgardens.com. Open year-round daily 9am–dusk. Call for holiday hours. $17 ($25 summer).

When you see these spectacular gardens, you'll be hard-pressed to imagine that this site was once a gaping quarry. In 1904 Jennie Butchart had a vision for the chasm in the ground left by her husband's quarrying operations. The 20ha/50 acres of gardens that resulted have achieved world fame for their splendour and variety. Still operated by the Butchart family, the gardens are among Canada's most popular attractions.

Sunken Garden – The justly famed and oft-pictured heart of the old quarry is the centrepiece garden. Green lawns curve around carefully tended masses of bright annuals, perennials and bulbs. The displays change with the season, and even winter has its blooms.

Ross Fountain – Within a rocky pool at the south end of the Sunken Garden, dramatic water displays feature changing patterns and, at night, an array of coloured lights.

Rose Garden – This popular plot holds a maze of bloom-covered arbors in peak season *(Jun–Sept)*, attracting rose lovers from around the world.

Japanese Garden – A secluded spot, the garden features exquisite lacquered bridges and wooden teahouses.

Italian Garden – This formal garden boasts statuary and a star-shaped lily pond surrounded by colourful plantings.

Tips for Visiting

Butchart's popularity has its drawbacks: peak summer days can find more than 50 tour buses in the huge parking lot, and the crowded paths can dampen your experience somewhat. Garden managers do what they can to minimize the effects of crowding (smoking is forbidden, for instance) but it's best to arrive early, or visit in spring and fall. In summer however, a fireworks display lights up the sky on Saturday nights. For a small re-admission fee ($3) you can return the following day to spread your visit over two days.

The on-site store sells a vast array of books devoted to gardening, botany and horticulture, as well as souvenirs and gift items. There is also a restaurant on the premises.

Royal British Columbia Museum★★★

675 Belleville St. 250-356-7226 or 888-447-7977. www.royalbcmuseum.bc.ca. Open year-round daily 9am–5pm. Closed Jan 1 & Dec 25. $14.

You could easily spend a day at Canada's most-visited museum. The Royal BC focuses on the natural and human history of the province, and is most noted for its depiction of First Nations life past and present.

First Peoples Exhibits – The **totems** on the first and third floors range from well-weathered historic pieces gathered at coastal villages in the 19C, to stunning 20C works carved by artists such as Bill Reid *(see Museums)* and Mungo Martin. Faced with the graceful, geometric forms used to represent ravens, bears, eagles, whales and other natural icons of coastal Native life, the totems exude as much power and presence in the museum halls as they did greeting visitors to seaside villages 150 years ago.

Two dozen **ceremonial masks**, representing every coastal Native carving style, are stunningly displayed in a dark case where each spotlit mask seems suspended in air. Audio and video presentations depict the ongoing struggle of BC's indigenous peoples to adapt to the modern world, including the restoration of the **potlatch tradition** (in which the masks are used by dancers) that was banned by British authorities in the late 19C. Stroll through the **longhouse** and peer into the **pit house** to gain an appreciation for the lifestyles of the Native American inhabitants.

Old Town – On the rest of the third floor you can walk the streets of a pioneer "Old Town"; poke your way through a coal mine (Vancouver Island's early prosperity derived from coal); and clamber around a replica of the *Discovery*, the ship George Vancouver sailed into BC waters in the late 18C.

Thunderbird Park

Adjacent to the museum at Belleville & Douglas Sts. This park has yet more totems, together with a longhouse in which Native carvers demonstrate their craft during the summer.

Natural History – Exceptional **dioramas** on the second floor illustrate the province's varied ecosystems, from temperate rain forest to interior desert. The museum is also a prominent stopping point for international exhibits, such as Egyptian antiquities, that sometimes visit no other North American venues.

Empress Hotel★★

721 Government St. 250-384-8111 or 800-257-7544. www.fairmont.com/empress.

Ah, the Empress, symbol of gentility. Designed by famed colonial architect Francis Rattenbury, this massive neo-Gothic granite landmark anchors Victoria's Inner Harbour. Since its 1908 opening, the Empress has epitomized the civility of the empire whose last days it witnessed. Over the years, this grande dame of hospitality has hosted royalty, celebrities, elite travellers and countless honeymooners. The hotel's public spaces include a vast Edwardian lobby; the glass-ceilinged Victorian **Palm Court**; the **Crystal Ballroom**; several clubby, dark-wood restaurants, lounges and sitting rooms; and the **Bengal Lounge**, whose colonial artifacts include tiger skins given to the hotel by the Thai royal family when they visited in the 1930s. Built by Canadian Pacific Railway as the westernmost property in its continent-wide chain of chateau hotels, the Empress is now operated by CP's successor, the Fairmont group *(see Must Stay).*

The Cougar Incident – As if to prove conclusively that no amount of civilizing can utterly tame Vancouver Island, one of the wildest of island creatures, a cougar, was discovered in the heart of Victorian urbanity—the Empress Hotel parking garage—in 1992. The garage gates were closed, wildlife officials called, and the cougar was tranquilized and returned to the wild. Victoria author Julie Lawson used the incident as the basis for a popular children's book, *In Like a Lion*—copies are, of course, available at the Empress news shop. Vancouver Island is considered by some wildlife experts to have the greatest density of mountain lions on earth.

Tea at the Empress

Victorian matrons, no doubt smartly attired, were the first patrons when the Empress began its famous tea service back in 1908. Today both the dress code and the service have become less formal (no shorts though, please), but the atmosphere remains largely the same. Served in the hotel's elegant, high-ceilinged lobby, or in the Palm Court, afternoon tea is offered at five sittings a day. Traditional finger sandwiches, scones, crumpets, heavy cream and berry preserves are presented, along with the Empress's own proprietary tea blend. It's not cheap—figure up to $40 a person. *Reservations are essential: 250-389-2727.*

Fort Rodd Hill National Historic Site★★

603 Fort Rodd Hill Rd. 14km/9mi west of Victoria via Rtes. 1, 1A and Ocean Blvd. 250-478-5849. www.pc.gc.ca/lhn-nhs/bc/fortroddhill. Open mid-Feb–Oct daily 10am–5:30pm. Rest of the year daily 9am–4:30pm. Closed Dec 25. $4.

Set on 18ha/44 acres of land at the southwest corner of Esquimalt's harbour, this fort defended Victoria and the nearby Esquimalt naval base from 1878 until 1956. Today the ruins of three coastal artillery gun batteries remain to tell the tale. Wander through the guardhouses, barracks and magazines to get a feel for day-to-day life in the garrison way back when.

Built in 1860, **Fisgard Lighthouse** was the first permanent light on the west coast of Canada; the house where the light's keeper once lived now contains exhibits and videos relating to the site. Here you'll also have great **views★** of Juan de Fuca Strait and the Olympic Mountains.

Scenic Marine Drive★★

Begin at Thunderbird Park, Douglas & Belleville Sts.

This beautiful drive reveals Victoria's splendid setting on the Strait of Juan de Fuca, yielding views of the city's gardens, neighbourhoods and scenic vistas. Start at Thunderbird Park, and head south on Douglas Street, past Beacon Hill Park and a plaque noting the starting point of Highway 1, the Trans-Canada Highway. Turn left on Dallas Road, heading east along the water. At Finlayson and Cover Points, stop to enjoy the panoramas of the strait, with the snow-capped Olympic Mountains in Washington State in the distance.

Centre of the Universe★

5071 W. Saanich Rd. Travel north on Hwy. 17A to Little Saanich Mountain. 250-363-8262. www.hia-iha.nrc-cnrc.gc.ca/cu. Open Apr–Oct daily 10am–6pm (Fri–Sun until 11pm). Rest of the year Tue–Fri 1pm–4:30pm, Sat 10am–4:30pm. $9.

In 1918, when it first went into service, this observatory's 1.6m/65in telescope was the largest in the world. No longer, of course, but it has one inestimable distinction today: visitors are allowed to actually turn the instrument themselves. On clear nights, vast celestial views abound; the nearby interpretive centre features intriguing displays about Canadian contributions to heavenly exploration.

Craigdarroch Castle★

1050 Joan Crescent. 250-592-5323. www.craigdarrochcastle.com. Open mid-Jun–Labour Day daily 9am–7pm, rest of year daily 10am–4:30pm. Closed Jan 1 & Dec 25–26. $11.50.

Scottish immigrant Robert Dunsmuir was BC's first tycoon, a coal baron who meant this castle to be the most grandiose home on North America's Pacific coast. The mansion was finished in the late 1890s, but, in an irony of biblical proportions, Dunsmuir was never able to glory in his creation—he died before it was done. The four-storey sandstone, granite and marble structure, complete with turrets and towers, shelters an opulent interior. Inside, meticulously hand-carved walls and intricate ceiling panelling greet visitors. Numerous ceiling-high stained-glass panels outshine all but the world's biggest cathedrals. The 87 steps of the massive oak stairway lead to a fourth floor ballroom.

Government Street★

Victoria's principal thoroughfare in Old Town is also its main shopping street, with five venerable stores that are destinations in themselves. Be sure to poke your head in at least one of them.

- **Rogers Chocolates** *(no. 913; 250-384-7021; www.rogerschocolates.com)* occupies a 1903 building with tile floors and oak display cases; the company began making its classic British-style truffles and candies in 1885. "Victoria creams" are Rogers' signature confection.

- **The Edinburgh Tartan Shop** *(no. 921; 250-953-7790)* presents its namesake Scottish textiles, plus an excellent selection of wool goods ranging from fine suits to kilts.

- **Murchie's Teas** *(no. 1110; 250-383-3112; www.murchies.com)* dates the beginnings of its business back to colonial days, when clipper ships called from Hong Kong with tea bales on board. (Remember all the trouble that caused in Boston?) Like its counterpart branch in Vancouver, teas here range from everyday orange pekoe to $99-an-ounce handpicked blends that, believe it or not, are good enough to justify the cost.

- **Munro's Books** *(no. 1108; 250-382-2464; www.munrobooks.com)* sits next door to Murchie's in an elegant late-19C bank building, with high, pressed-tin ceilings. Munro's selection of BC books is superlative.

- **Old Morris Tobacconist** *(no. 1116; 250-382-4811; www.oldmorris.com)* has a heady array of pipe tobaccos, which, signifying the store's British leanings, are stored in the humidor. The cigars are out in the open, and yes, Cuban cigars number among the selection.

Helmcken House★

675 Belleville Street. 250-356-7226 www.royalbcmuseum.bc.ca. Open for special events; call or check museum Web site.

This house, located behind the Royal BC Museum, is the restored 1852 home of Victoria pioneer doctor J.S. Helmcken, who served as physician to the Hudson's Bay Company at Fort Victoria. The doctor and his wife raised their seven children in this dwelling. Rooms are decorated in period furnishings brought around Cape Horn on clipper ships to Victoria; his medical equipment is also on display.

Maritime Museum of British Columbia★

28 Bastion Square. 250-385-4222. www.mmbc.bc.ca. Open summer daily 9:30am–5pm, rest of year to 4:30pm. $8.

You'll recognise this building by the lighthouse beacon outside it. Housed in the old courthouse, the maritime museum presents an eclectic collection of maps, artifacts, charts and model ships that depicts the province's seafaring past. Two small boats—a traditional dugout canoe and a ketch—offer up-close evidence of the adventurous spirit of the early mariners.

Parliament Buildings★

501 Belleville St..250-387-3046. Open Jun–Labour Day daily 9am–5pm. Rest of the year Mon–Fri 9am–4pm.

Intended to reflect the character, if not the actual majesty, of London's Parliament, this complex was designed by Francis Rattenbury, architect of the Empress Hotel. He blended (critics say he "mashed together") Victorian, Romanesque and Italianate design elements, including 33 copper domes, to create a complex that is one of Victoria's visual icons. The BC Legislature is in session here in winter and spring; guided tours explain the sometimes inexplicable workings of BC government, as well as the building's history. And what would a building of British heritage be without statues? An image of Queen Victoria stands out front, and Captain George Vancouver's likeness tops the highest dome.

Francis Rattenbury

Francis Mawson Rattenbury (1867–1935) lived a life as colourful as his famous designs are grandiose. Born in England, he achieved modest success as an architect until he moved to BC and wangled the commission to design Victoria's Parliament Buildings in the late 1890s. That got him hired by Canadian Pacific folks, who set him to work designing the Empress Hotel. Rattenbury cut quite a figure in BC society, until the revelation of an affair with Alma Pakenham, who was 30 years his junior, drove both from the New World back to the Old. There Rattenbury was murdered; Alma and her new lover were charged. He was sentenced to life in prison, and she committed suicide.

Chinatown

Bounded by Pandora Ave., Herald, Government & Store Sts.

Encompassing two city blocks, Victoria's Chinatown, though much smaller in scale than Vancouver's, has much the same flavour—tea, herb and spice shops; stalls with exotic produce; Asian imports stores; and dim sum restaurants. The entrance to Chinatown is marked by the 1981 **Gate of Harmonious Interest**, a lavishly figured, vividly coloured archway over Fisgard Street at Government. **Fan Tan Alley**, just .9m/3ft wide at its narrowest, is a warren of small shops. Once this district harboured gambling and opium dens.

- **Silk Road** – *1624 Government St. 250-388-6815. www.silkroadtea.com.* Get a whiff of this superlative tea and bath shop in Chinatown, which proffers bath salts and soaps containing exotic herbs and oils, such as fir and geranium.

Emily Carr House

207 Government St. 250-383-5843. www.emilycarr.com. Open May–Sept daily 11am–4pm; closed Sun–Mon in May & Sept. Call for Christmas season hours.

The tidy Victorian home in which famed British Columbia artist Emily Carr (1871–1917) grew up is furnished as it was during her girlhood. Her journals have guided the reconstruction of the gardens to appear as they did a century ago. Carr's unique portrayals of West Coast landscapes and First Nations villages manifested her reverence for nature and Native culture *(see Museums)*.

Victoria's Blossom Count

Victoria has long claimed the mildest climate in Canada—a claim it renews each spring during the city's annual blossom count in late February. Residents are invited to count the flower blooms—daffodils, azaleas, camellias—in their yards, and report the number to volunteers who man special phone lines. All the blossoms are added up at the end of a week (theoretically, all the counts are totally accurate, and no one phones in more than once) and the grand total is publicized, with great fanfare, across Canada. The total is invariably huge—and it doesn't even include Butchart Gardens. While Calgarians and Ontarians are shoveling snow, Victoria's residents are enjoying two to four billion flowers. Yes, that's a "b"—for billion.

Government House

1401 Rockland Ave. 250-387-2080.

This baronial stone mansion is the official residence of the lieutenant-governor, who represents the Queen in British Columbia. The exquisitely landscaped grounds, including rose, herb and perennial gardens, are open to the public for uncrowded strolling dawn to dusk.

Inner Harbour

Along Wharf St.

The heart of Victoria edges this lively, boat and floatplane-filled harbour, with the Empress Hotel directly ahead, the Parliament Buildings to one side, and Old Town to the other. Here, on a summer day, fresh breezes blow off the water, street musicians ply their craft on stone benches, hanging baskets of petunias and geraniums glisten in the sun, and you could almost swear it was the year 1900.

Tourism Victoria's main **Infocentre** is located at the west end of the Inner Harbour *(812 Wharf St.; 250-953-2033; www.tourismvictoria.com; open early Sept–May daily 9am–8:30pm; rest of the year daily 9am–5pm).*

An Empire of Antiques

Just as colonial civil servants wended their way to Victoria to retire, so did their bric-a-brac possessions. That was long ago, of course, but the tradition of selling antiques in this city has as much heritage as any of its Victorian buildings. Today almost all the finer antique stores are concentrated in a three-block stretch of **Fort Street**, from Blanshard Street uphill to Cook. Here you can find anything from rare Burmese tapestries to early rock 'n roll 45s (if you even remember what those are!), and the selection of silverware, crystal and crockery is exceptional. Here's a sampling of shops:

- **Romanoff & Company** *(837 Fort St.; 250-480-1543)* has thousands of pieces of exquisite china and dinnerware.
- **Wells Books** *(824 Fort St.; 250-360-2929)* carries countless rare volumes and specializes in nautical texts.
- **Antiquarian Print Room** *(840 Fort St.; 250-380-1343)* focuses on maps and prints from the Victorian era and earlier.

Pacific Rim National Park Reserve★★★

Follow Hwy. 1 north from Victoria to Parksville, then take Hwy. 4 west, through Port Alberni to the park. 250-726-7721. www.pc.gc.ca/pn-np/bc/pacificrim. Open daily year-round, but park facilities are closed mid-Oct–mid-Mar. $6.90.

Wave-tossed rocky headlands, lengthy sand beaches, deep old-growth spruce forests and a beautiful inland sound with untouched islands are just some of the natural elements that make up this outstanding natural preserve. Hugging the West Coast of Vancouver Island, Pacific Rim National Park includes three distinct units: Long Beach, Broken Group Islands and West Coast Trail. The park's **visitor centre** *(open mid-Mar–mid-Oct daily 9am–6pm; 250-726-4212)* is located just past the junction where Highway 4 turns north.

Long Beach★★ – Stretching from just north of Ucluelet in the south, where Highway 4 turns north, northward to within 4.8km/3mi of Tofino, this area is the only part of the park reachable by a road. The namesake beach has almost 32km/20mi of shoreline, most of it open beach, with firm gray sand for strolling, dozens of offshore sea stacks to send waves crashing upward, and open expanses where the perfect curls of breaking waves draw dozens of surfers (Tofino is the surfing capital of Canada).

Radar Hill★★ – *About 29km/18mi north of the visitor centre.* The 91m/300ft summit (highest on this stretch of coast) of this hill affords a 360-degree **panorama★★** of the ocean and the island behind. The road ends in **Tofino★**, 33.5km/21mi from the Ucluelet junction.

Broken Group Islands – The second unit, composed of more than 100 islands, is contained entirely within **Barkley Sound**, a small inland sound south of Ucluelet. It is one of the premier saltwater kayaking areas on earth. Permits are required to visit the islands; outfitting and transport to the sound is available in Ucluelet.

West Coast Trail – This legendary 75km/47mi wilderness trail traverses the coast between Bamfield and Port Renfrew. The arduous trek takes up to six days, the weather is notoriously temperamental, and reservations are neces-sary long in advance, as park officials limit yearly use to about 8,000 hikers.

Wickaninnish Centre – *At end of Wick Rd., 8km/5mi north of the visitor centre. Open mid-Mar–mid-Oct daily 9am–6pm.* This interpretive facility explains the North Pacific ecosystem, including the life cycles of the gray whales that pass just offshore during their annual migration between Alaska and Mexico.

Must Sees Near Pacific Rim National Park

Hot Springs Cove★

North of Tofino; access by boat only. Charters leave Tofino year-round.

Few places anywhere on earth offer what this legendary provincial park does: an unparalleled sensory experience for bathers. The hot spring waters arise in a headland about 61m/200ft inland and spill down the rocky channel to the Pacific waters of Clayoquot Sound. You can sit in the hot water pools and let the cold sea water wash over you as waves arrive. The view out over the ocean, the salt breeze, and the peaceful wilderness surroundings all combine to make one of the most memorable experiences of a lifetime. It's best to come here during the week in spring and fall, when crowds are low. Along the way, you might see whales, dolphins, sea lions and eagles. **Jamie's Whaling Station** is the leading tour operator in Tofino *(606 Campbell St.; 250-725-3919 or 800-667-9913; www.jamies.com).*

Tofino★

At the end of northern end of Hwy. 4, on Long Beach peninsula.

This small harbour receives more than one million visitors in summer. Erstwhile logging and fishing capital, Tofino is popular as a surfing centre. The community's central role in the Clayoquot Sound logging furor has brought it a distinct countercultural flavour. You'll often see barefooted youths traipsing through town with hefty packs, just as you'll see pickup trucks piled high with fishing nets, and family vans with tourists. Tofino hardly attracted anyone in winter until the opening of Wickaninnish Inn *(see Must Stay)* kicked off the storm-watching aspect of the coastal visitor industry. Whale-watching, surfing, upscale accommodations, national-park camping, commercial fishing, and holdover logging—it's a heady cultural mix in this little town, and that's part of its unique character.

Ancient Cedars Spa

At the Wickaninnish Inn, Chesterman Beach, Tofino. 250-725-3100 or 800-333-4604. www.wickinn.com. 76 rooms. Located on the lower level of the oceanside lodge near Pacific Rim National Park, the spa at the Wickaninnish Inn sports a saltwater theme, utilizing thalassotherapy, seaweed wraps, sea-salt scrubs and the like to reflect the environment just out the door. The surroundings are exquisite—a leisurely hour-long walk on the long, sandy beach is the perfect way to conclude an afternoon of spa pampering.

Clayoquot Sound – Pocked by dozens of small islands, this vast body of in-shore saltwater northeast of Tofino has a fascinating modern cultural history. Settlement on the sound began with a Nootka band under the leadership of Chief Wickaninnish. In the 20C, plans to turn the sound's forests over to timber companies for clear-cutting provoked an international outcry that attracted protestors from around the world, especially Europe. At one point, demonstrators seized the bridge over the Kennedy River and blocked traffic on Highway 4 for two days. The uproar eventually forced the provincial government to back down, and all interested parties—timber companies, environmental activists, First Nations bands and local residents—hammered out an agreement that allows limited selective logging in the area, but not clear-cutting. The whole story, along with the delicate balance of life in the rain forest ecosystem, is told at the **Rainforest Interpretive Centre** in Tofino *(451 Main St.; 250-725-2560, www.tofinores.com)*.

Hanging Garden Tree – *Along the main hiking path on Meares Island, just east of Tofino in Clayoquot Sound. Access by water taxi from Tofino.* Here's a natural sight that's worth a 20-minute hike: the 1,000-year-old Hanging Garden Tree. This much-photographed Western red cedar has been worn down over time into a bulky 30m/100ft vertical burl with numerous side-limbs and a base broad enough to anchor a suspension bridge. The cracks and shoulders along the trunk have accumulated debris, which decayed into soil and sprouted wind-blown seeds. Today you have a tree that is host to dozens of other growing things. The Hanging Garden Tree became a visual symbol for the early 1990s campaign to protect the sound's forest from clear-cutting. The controversy has muted now, and the tree remains.

More Must Sees on Vancouver Island

Cathedral Grove★★

Along Highway 4, about 16 km/10mi west of Parksville.

One of the last remaining old-growth groves on lower Vancouver Island was given to the province by lumber baron H.R. MacMillan. The Douglas firs in this magnificent grove approach 75m/250ft in height and 1,000 years in age. Short hiking trails lead from the highway (which splits the grove) into the woods; an elevated walkway affords a good view of the devastation caused by a fierce windstorm in the mid-1990s.

Cowichan Valley

On Hwy. 1, about 80km/50mi north of Victoria.

As Highway 1 leaves Victoria, it climbs a steep grade called Malahat Mountain, atop which viewpoints afford sensational vistas of the Gulf Islands and San Juan Islands, with the US mainland's snowcapped Mount Baker in the distance. The road then descends to sea level, entering the valley of the Cowichan River. The name is an attempt to translate a Native word that means "warm land," a reflection of the area's benign climate.

That climate has led to the development of a nascent wine-growing district. Most of the vineyards are fairly young, and viticulturists and winemakers are still learning the eccentricities of their climate (it may be warm, but it's not California). The area's road network is a farm-country maze, so it's best to phone for directions to the following wineries:

- **Vignetti Zanatta** *(5039 Marshall Rd., Duncan; 250-748-2338; www.zanatta.ca)*, oldest in the district, it also has a fine restaurant in a heritage farmhouse.

- **Cherry Point Vineyards** *(840 Cherry Point Rd., Cobble Hill; 250-743-1272; www.cherrypointvineyards.com)* has a tasting room that's open daily.

- **Blue Grouse Vineyards** *(4365 Blue Grouse Rd., Duncan; 250-743-3834; www.bluegrousevineyards.com)* is a family-run winery with a tasting room open four days a week.

- **Merridale Cidery** *(1230 Merridale Rd., Cobble Hill; 250-743-4293; www.merridalecider.com)* is the leading West Coast orchard, with more than 4ha/10 acres planted with hundreds of apple trees—they pioneered hard-cider making in the West. Visitors are welcome year-round *(call for hours)*, but the best time to stop by is in September and October, when daily pressings produce gallons upon gallons of highly flavoured juice.

The Aerie

35km/22mi north of Victoria, about .8km/.5mi off Hwy. 1, in Malahat. 250-743-7115 or 800-518-1933. www.aerie.bc.ca.

Perched on a ridge above Highway 1—and high above the Victoria area—this pricey overnight accommodation is extravagant in every way. Its Mediterranean design seems incongruous amid the conifer rain forest in which it sits; the stucco complex looks like nothing so much as an Aegean resort. All suites, the guest rooms are opulent in the extreme, with brocade fabrics, rich colors and platform beds. The dining room specializes in sumptuous meals that feature exotic ingredients like fiddlehead ferns and sea urchins. As one guest put it, this is a place that belongs in the movies.

Juan de Fuca Provincial Park

On Hwy. 14, west of Sooke. 250-391-2300. www.env.gov.bc.ca/bcparks. Open year-round daily dawn–dusk.

This shoreline preserve runs from the Jordan River to Port Renfrew—in some places stretching less than half a kilometre (.25mi) inland from the beach. A multifaceted wonder, the park offers different levels of experience of the West Coast of Vancouver Island. Four access points allow easy hikes down to the shore, where Pacific breakers roll in on pebble-sand beaches; trails descend through old-growth Sitka spruce, massive trees with gnarled branches that may remind you of J.R.R. Tolkien's tree creatures, the "ents." **China Beach**, the first access, and **Botanical Beach**, the most distant *(2 ½ hours from Victoria)* are the best beaches. At the latter, low tide reveals a broad expanse of tide pools in which anemones unfurl, nudibranchs shimmer, and starfish splash vivid orange and purple on the rocks.

Whale Watching off Vancouver Island

The whales that ply the inland and coastal waters of the Pacific Northwest are among North America's most beloved wild creatures. Thousands of sightseers board boats daily to head out in hopes of a glimpse of graceful black-and-white orcas slipping through the Georgia Strait, or the much bigger gray whales that migrate north and south along the Pacific coast between Alaska and Mexico. These cruises are among the most popular of visitor activities, but controversy accompanies them.

Some conservation advocates (and some scientists) believe the unremitting presence of dozens of noisy boats interferes with the whales' daily lives, especially the orcas, who use sound waves to communicate and to locate prey. The three Puget Sound killer-whale pods, in particular, are in decline, though scientists debate the reasons why.

You can see whales from many shoreline points, such as those in Victoria's Oak Bay neighbourhood, though sightings cannot be guaranteed. Be sure the boat you board subscribes to the industry's code of ethics, which forbids chasing whales, and prescribes a minimum distance between boats and whales.

For referrals to whale-watching companies that adhere to the code of ethics, contact Victoria Tourism *(250-953-2033; www.tourismvictoria.com). For information about whale-watching cruises from Vancouver, see Musts for Outdoor Fun.*

Whistler★★

Take Hwy. 1 in West Vancouver west to Horseshoe Bay, then follow Hwy. 99 north about 102km/63mi. Tourist information: Whistler Tourism Centre, 4010 Whistler Way; 604-938-2769 or 877-991-9988; www.tourismwhistler.com.

Less than 45 years old, Whistler today is one of the largest and most popular ski resorts in the world. Nonetheless it confines itself to a relatively compact developed area in a bowl-shaped valley deep within the Coast Range. The community has adopted a "bed cap" that limits residential and hospitality growth, since this year-round resort attracts visitors in all seasons, not just when there's snow on the ground.

What's In Whistler If You Don't Ski?

Fabulous dining, shopping, nightclubbing and spa pampering 12 months a year. Hiking, biking, golf, canoeing, rafting, ballooning, fishing, climbing and horseback riding in summer; in winter there's ice skating, dogsledding, tubing, Nordic skiing and snowmobiling.

What's In Whistler If You Do Ski?

Two mountains that, combined, appear at the top of most ski resort ratings every year. No other area in North America has as great a vertical drop—1,609m/5,280ft. No other area has as long a season—skiing continues on the Blackcomb Glacier until August, and would go year-round except that, frankly, no one's interested for that long. When Whistler advertises itself as a full-service resort, it's not kidding: Where else can you buy a ski/golf package that allows you to work on carving your turns in the morning, and curbing your slice in the afternoon?

Skiing Whistler and Blackcomb

The season runs roughly November to April. Fourteen high-speed lifts can carry 52,000 skiers an hour to the top of **Blackcomb Mountain** and **Whistler Mountain**, two nearly identical peaks that face each other across a small valley. Annual snowfall averages 9m/30ft, and since the valley is clasped within the middle of the Coast Range 80km/50mi from Howe Sound, the snow is not as wet and heavy as at Northwest resorts directly facing the ocean. There are 200 trails, 12 bowls and three glaciers in 2,833ha/7,000 acres of skiable terrain—the longest intermediate run stretches a luxurious 11km/7mi. The base is at 670.5m/2,200ft, and skiing tops out at about 2,286m/7,500ft on both mountains. One lift ticket covers both, $77 in high season.

Whistler in Summer

In summer the area's setting and character draw large numbers of visitors for numerous outdoor activities.

Mountain Peeking – Try the view from above. Take the **Whistler Gondola** *(open late-Jun–late-Sept daily 10am–4pm)* for a ride to the top *($30)*; you can even include a barbecue lunch at the mountaintop restaurant.

Biking – Energetic visitors rent mountain bikes at the **Garbanzo Bike & Bean Shop** *(at the foot of the lift; 604-905-2076)* and ride all the way down Whistler—the descent takes about three hours. Ride or bike down—you'll enjoy magnificent panoramas of numerous Coast Range peaks in every direction.

Canoeing and River Running – **Whistler Outdoor Experience** *(604-932-3389; www.whistleroutdoor.com)* rents equipment and provides guided tours for canoe trips on clear, cold **Green Lake** *(8km/5mi east of Whistler Village)*, and sponsors guided kayak and canoe trips down the River of Golden Dreams—yes, that really *is* its name.

Golf – The **Chateau Whistler Golf Club** *(604-938-2092; www.fairmontchateau-whistlergolfclub.com)* was designed by Robert Trent Jones, Jr.; the 122m/400ft elevation gain along the course is softened by the GPS computers onboard the carts. **Nicklaus North** *(604-896-2224; www.golfbc.com/courses/furry_creek)*, designed by Jack Nicklaus, winds around Green Lake.

Fishing – In minutes, helicopters can whisk visitors to alpine wilderness lakes; guides help you decide what fly to cast where. For information, contact **Whistler Backcountry Adventures**: *604-932-3474.*

Winter Olympics 2010

Whistler's founders in the early 1960s dreamed that one day the area would host a Winter Olympics. The fantasy came true in July 2003 when, in tandem with Vancouver, the 2010 winter games were awarded to the region. Among the area's virtues that appealed to the International Olympic committee is the fact that Whistler can handle an event of such global proportions with relatively modest preparation.

Alpine events—downhill skiing, bobsledding, ski jumping—will take place on Whistler and Blackcomb mountains. A bobsled and luge facility will be built, but existing lifts and other facilities are adequate as is. A Nordic ski centre will be built in a nearby valley, adding to Whistler's overall appeal for years to come.

Snowboarding, freestyle skiing, skating, hockey and all the other winter Olympic events will take place in the Vancouver area. Not only is Whistler not big enough to handle all those activities, it didn't want to.

Okanagan Valley★★

From Vancouver, follow Hwy. 1 east, then take Hwy. 5 (the Coquihalla Hwy.) northeast ($10 toll at the top), then take Hwy. 97C & Hwy. 97 east to Kelowna.

Clasped between towering highlands on either side, the Okanagan Valley runs north-south along its namesake lake and river—a geographic happenstance that has resulted in a sun-rich climate perfect for growing fruits and vegetables (an industry that dates back to the mid-19C). The climate is also perfect for growing retirement communities. Modern development of subdivisions, golf courses and shopping centres has begun to threaten the viability of the region's longstanding agricultural community.

Okanagan Lake★★

Monsters unknown to science ply the 305m/1,000ft deep waters of this 121km/75mi-long spring-fed lake. So goes the legend, anyway; local officials have periodically offered a million-dollar reward to anyone who acquires incontrovertible proof that **Ogopogo** actually exists. So far, the closest claimant turned out to be a video of an extra-large beaver.

The lake is a geographic and recreational marvel—it never freezes; it has so far withstood the pollution of urban development; and it hardly ever varies much in depth, though its lower end has just a modest weir leading to its outflow. Boaters, canoeists, sailors, anglers, sailboarders and swimmers all enjoy its waters, as do countless waterfowl.

When you come down from the Okanagan Highlands on Highway 97C, the first sight of the sparkling blue lake is one of the more memorable vistas in BC. Ogopogo or no, this lake needs no exotic sea monster to embellish its wonder.

U-pick Farms

For decades Canadian families have hopped in their cars and driven to the Okanagan to pick their own. Fruits and vegetables are available at dozens of small farms throughout the valley—from Vernon in the north to Osoyoos in the south, though most are between Penticton (an hour south of Kelowna) and Oliver, a half-hour farther south, along Highway 97. To find a U-pick farm, simply watch by the road for signs, and decide what you want. Peaches, apricots, nectarines, plums, pears, apples, strawberries, raspberries and blueberries are the major fruits; vegetables range from asparagus to zucchini, with tomatoes, corn and chilis especially popular. Prices are per pound, in the sack—the custom is that whatever you sample on-site is free. Many orchards offer picnic facilities for families who make a day trip of their fruit-picking journeys.

O'Keefe Ranch★★

Northwest of Vernon, on Hwy. 97, at the northern end of Okanagan Lake. 250-542-7868. www.okeeferanch.bc.ca. Open May–Oct daily 9am–6pm. $10.

It's easy to see why Cornelius O'Keefe decided to stop here while driving cattle through the valley in the 1860s. The bunchgrass grew as high as a horse's belly, the breeze off the lake moderated the summer heat, and the setting is as bucolic as any you're likely to see. The ranch he built became one of the largest and most prosperous, with dozens of houses, shops, outbuildings and residents. Today this BC Heritage site is the largest such historic ranch in Western Canada, with something for everyone. The **General Store** is stocked with goods from the turn of the 19C. The **O'Keefe Mansion** is an elegant late-Victorian house with cut glass, wood trim and front and back stairs (the latter were for noisy children). Come for the annual **Cowboy Festival** in late July; it's a real rodeo, with cow-hands from nearby ranches competing for prizes and bragging rights.

Desert Interpretive Centre★

3km/2mi north of Osoyoos on Hwy. 87. 250-495-2470 or 877-899-0897. www.desert.org. Open May–Oct daily 10am–4pm, extended hours Jun–Aug. $6.

The southern interior of BC contains Canada's only non-polar desert, and this preserve, established in the late 1990s, is designed to accomplish two aims: help protect the desert, and help people understand why it's important. Take a guided tour along the boardwalk through the sagebrush and sand landscape; along the way, naturalists explain the hardy creatures that thrive in this challenging ecosystem, such as endangered rattlesnakes and burrowing owls.

Keremeos Grist Mill★

Upper Bench Rd., just off Hwy. 3A, in Keremeos. 43km/27mi southwest of Penticton. 250-499-2888. www.keremeos.com/gristmill. Open daily May–Oct daily 9am–5pm.

First opened in 1877, this restored mill occupies a pleasant, pastoral spot in a sensationally beautiful upland valley along the **Similkameen River**. Tall cottonwoods line the streambanks, including the small freshet that turns the grindstone (yes, it's really stone) in the gristmill. Now a BC Heritage site, the mill grinds flour just as it did more than a century ago. The gift shop sells the mill's flour, ground using grains from the Prairie provinces; the flour makes great pancakes, cornbread and muffins.

Kelowna★

395km/245mi east of Vancouver via Hwy. 1 East to Hwy. 5 North to Hwy. 97C South.

The biggest city in the BC interior (metro area population is about 250,000) is a small, thriving metropolis whose agricultural past is being augmented by high-tech industry and tourism. The city's resorts rely on Okanagan Lake's proximity and the valley's dependably warm summers for their existence; the burgeoning wine industry has become a significant draw as well.

The first European settler in the area was Father Charles Pandosy, an Oblate friar who established a mission along a creek in 1860. The remarkable houses and barns he built of hand-hewn cottonwoods—artfully joined by dovetail notching—still stand at **Pandosy Mission Provincial Heritage Site★** *(Benvoulin & Casorso Rds., east Kelowna; www.okanaganhistoricalsociety.org).*

The rest of Kelowna's past is on view at a complex of museums downtown, chief among which describe the viticulture and orcharding industries.

- **Orchard Museum** – *470 Queensway Ave. 250-763-2417. www.kelownamuseum.ca. Open year-round Mon–Sat 10am–5pm. Closed major holidays.* Here you'll see how the industry's development depended on transportation to get the fruit to market—by boat along the lake to a railhead, then on to Vancouver. One of the museum's most delightful aspects is the collection of Art Deco-style fruit-box labels.

- **Wine Museum** – *1304 Ellis St. 250-868-0441. www.kelownamuseum.ca. Open year-round Mon–Fri 10am–6pm, Sat 10am–5pm, Sun & holidays 11am–5pm. Closed Jan 1, Dec 25-26.* Exhibits describe how pioneers had to overcome skepticism about the industry's potential this far north; a selection of Okanagan wines is on sale in the adjacent shop.

Kelowna Land and Orchard

2930 Dunster Rd. 250-763-1091. www.k-l-o.com. Open Jun–Oct daily 9am–5pm. A few years ago, third-generation orchardist Rich Bullock was eyeing an old tractor on his family farm when he was struck by the idea of hooking up a wagon and offering tours through the orchard. Hundreds of visitors now hop on KLO's wagons for entertaining and informative trips ($6.50) through the family's 73ha/180-acre orchard. The KLO farm store offers produce grown in the adjacent fields, and the cafe serves soups, salads, sandwiches and of course, apple pie. Set on a bench above Kelowna, the whole enterprise has a spectacular view of the city, the lake and the surrounding mountains.

BC Wine Country

The warm summer climate and cool nights of the Okanagan Valley have proven ideal for growing wine grapes, and a happy accident (that at first seemed calamitous) led to the area's signature product. When one vineyard's grapes froze on the vines one fall, the winemaker let them thaw and fermented the juice into a sweet aperitif called ice wine—BC ice wines now enjoy huge popularity in Asia, and many grape crops are deliberately left on the vines to freeze.

Dozens of wineries now operate in the valley, mostly around Kelowna and in the arid valley south of Penticton. That city's **Wine Country Visitor Centre**, similar to the one in Napa, California, has winery pamphlets, touring maps, and a shop that sells an extensive selection of Okanagan wines *(553 Railway St., Penticton; 250-490-2006; www.bcwineinfo.net; open year-round daily 10am–6pm; extended hours in summer).*

Winning Wineries

Mission Hill Family Estate – *1730 Mission Hill Rd., in Westbank, 250-768-7611. www.missionhillwinery.com. Tastings & tours daily.* Aiming to become one of the top wineries on earth (no  small objective), this ambitious operation across the lake from Kelowna has invested millions of dollars in facilities—a large visitor centre, an outdoor performance amphitheatre, tasting rooms, dining rooms and extensive underground cellars. It's known for its chardonnay, merlot and ice wine.

Quail's Gate Estate Winery – *3303 Boucherie Rd., Kelowna. 250-769-4451 or 800-420-9463. www.quailsgate.com. Tastings & tours daily.* Located in a 130-year-old log home, Quail's Gate winery focuses on merlot, pinot noir and chardonnay.

Burrowing Owl Estate Winery – *100 Burrowing Owl Pl., Oliver. Tours daily May–Oct. 250-498-0620 or 877-498-0620. www.bovwine.com.* This winery is noted for its intensely flavoured reds. At the winery's Sonora Room restaurant, you can taste how Burrowing Owl's wines complement fine regional cuisine.

Tinhorn Creek – *On Road 7 in Oliver. 250-498-3743 or 888-484-6467. www.tinhorn.com. Self-guided tours & tastings daily 10am–5pm.* Nestled against the foothills on the west side of the valley, Tinhorn is famed for varietal reds such as merlot. Nearby Tinhorn Creek was the site of a 19C gold mine.

Must Eat: Vancouver Restaurants

The venues listed below were selected for their ambience, location and/or value for money. Rates indicate the average cost of an appetizer, an entrée and a dessert for one person (not including tax, gratuity or beverages). Most restaurants are open daily and accept major credit cards. Call for information regarding reservations, dress code and opening hours. Restaurants listed are located in Vancouver unless otherwise noted. For a complete listing of restaurants mentioned in this guide, see Index.

$$$$	over $75	**$$**	$25–$50
$$$	$50–$75	**$**	under $25

Luxury

Chartwell $$$$ Continental

791 W. Georgia St., in the Four Seasons Hotel. 604-689-9333. www.fourseasons.com/vancouver.

Designed to represent an English club, with overstuffed furniture, wood panelling and a crackling fireplace, Chartwell is a cozy, secluded bastion of continental dining. Here's a place where you can still get traditional lobster bisque, or steaks and chops grilled with béarnaise sauce. Desserts usually include bread pudding. The service is unusually expert.

Lumiere $$$$ French

2551 W. Broadway. Dinner only. Closed Mon. 604-739-8185. www.lumiere.ca.

Each night's prix-fixe dinners display chef Robert Feenie's innovative, skilled meshing of BC ingredients with classic French cuisine. The spare, white linen décor focuses attention on the food in this Canadian culinary shrine, often tabbed one of the top restaurants in the country. Though menus are seasonal, a typical meal might feature prawn tartare, squash-mascarpone ravioli, seared striped bass, pancetta-wrapped rabbit and beef tenderloin. A new tasting bar offers the chance to sample Feenie's cooking at a more economical price.

Moderate

Bacchus $$$ French

845 Hornby St., in the Wedgewood Hotel. 604-608-5319. www.wedgewoodhotel.com.

The ostensibly French cuisine here contains a strong hint of Northern Italy, as well—all the way up to the Venetian-glass lamps hanging over the tables. Roast rosemary-studded lamb, braised duck, cassoulet, and seared halibut typify the changing menu; crème brûlée in various incarnations (apricot, pear, etc.) is the dessert standout. The atmosphere is muted and refined, and smokers can retire to the enclosed cigar lounge after dinner.

Bishop's $$$ West Coast

2183 W. 4th Ave. Dinner only. 604-738-2025. www.bishopsonline.com.

John Bishop is widely credited with inaugurating modern fine dining in Vancouver when he opened his namesake restaurant in Kitsilano. Bishop himself still greets diners most nights, and such personable service distinguishes the low-key, white-tablecloth ambience. The menu is a changing array of West Coast innovation, typified by such cross-cultural entrées as duck confit with lentil cassoulet and roast parsnips, and chèvre cheesecake for dessert.

Blue Water Cafe $$$ Seafood

1095 Hamilton St. Dinner only. 604-688-8078. www.bluewatercafe.net.

Blue Water artfully melds the style and flair of a top-notch steakhouse with exceptional gourmet seafood. The signature dish is the appetizer tower, a multilevel set of trays with up to a dozen treats piled on it—shrimp, ahi tuna, oysters, crabcakes, roe, sushi rolls, clams, and so on. Many diners simply order this for dinner. Main dishes are expertly cooked fish filets, ranging from salmon to shark; save room for the lemon tart. Warm wood tones and side lighting create an elegant atmosphere in this reconfigured Yaletown warehouse.

C Restaurant
$$$ Seafood

1600 Howe St. 604-681-1164. www.crestaurant.com.

C chef and co-owner Robert Clark stood the seafood world on its head when he conjured up such unorthodox delicacies as seared scallops wrapped in octopus bacon. Smoked black cod (sablefish), whole fish steamed in tea, caviar wrapped in gold foil, and gorgonzola cheesecake number among the other signature dishes. The minimalist black and white décor is airy (a visit to the whimsically decorated bathrooms is a must) and the patio overlooking False Creek is the best seat in the house on sunny days.

Cioppino's Mediterranean Grill
$$$ Italian

1133 Hamilton St. 604-688-7466. www.cioppinosyaletown.com.

Attentive service reaches its peak at this high-end Yaletown bistro. The Italian cuisine is exceptional, with pastas, risottos and the namesake seafood stew weighting the menu. But what's most memorable is the array of waiters—up to a half-dozen per table—ready to spring to action. The open, exhibition kitchen seems impossibly busy, with a small army of cooks and waiters hustling in and out. Somehow it all works. This renovated warehouse features huge beams overhead, but the industrial feel is softened by cherry-wood trim.

Diva
$$$ West Coast

645 Howe St., in the Metropolitan Hotel. 604-602-7788. www.metropolitan.com/diva.

This glistening brass-and-glass restaurant is one of the birthplaces of Vancouver's West Coast cuisine. Several levels of well-lit dining floors make Diva a place to see and be seen; it's especially popular for pre-theatre dinners. Signature dishes include smoked black cod, gently braised. The after-dinner cheese course is one of the most extensive in North America, with a wide selection of European, American and Canadian artisan cheeses.

Fleuri
$$$ French

845 Burrard St., in the Sutton Place Hotel. 604-642-2900. www.vancouver.suttonplace.com.

Though the French menu here is one of the city's finest, this hotel dining room is best known for its food bars. Each night, the Choc-a-holic bar tempts diners with dozens of chocolate confections, from traditional Black Forest cake to rich truffles. Friday and Saturday nights, the Taste of

Atlantis seafood buffet features dozens of fish and shellfish preparations, all fresh. And the Sunday brunch buffet lays out breakfast, dinner, seafood and dessert dishes on several long tables—including a dangerously rich bread pudding made with croissants.

Imperial Chinese Seafood $$$ Mandarin

355 Burrard St. 604-688-8191. www.imperialrest.com.

With trim, white-cloth-covered tables looking out over Coal Harbour beneath a high, arched ceiling, this restaurant is one of the most elegant dining rooms in Vancouver. The Marine Building in which it is housed is a world-class Art Deco shrine. Cantonese fare matches the atmosphere—high-style dishes such as Peking duck, sautéed lobster and crab, and sizzling beef and pineapple. Dim sum is available at lunch.

Joe Fortes Seafood & Chop House $$$ Seafood

777 Thurlow St. 604-669-1940. www.joefortes.ca.

Joe's specialty is raw oysters—more than a dozen kinds on most nights, affording diners the chance to savour the taste differences between oysters grown in a variety of waters. The clubby, dark-wood atmosphere lends a chop house air to this West End haunt, and the best entrées are simply grilled or pan-seared filets of halibut, cod, salmon and rockfish. Hand-cut steaks and chops round out the meaty menu.

Parkside $$$ West Coast

1906 Haro St. Dinner only. 604-683-6912. www.parksiderestaurant.ca.

Only a couple of blocks from Stanley Park, Parkside is the place to go for a quiet late dinner—and on a warm summer evening, you'll want to linger over your food on the large patio. The menu changes daily and features a selection of different local starters, entrées and desserts: you can order à la carte, or prix-fixe for a selection from each category.

Budget

Cardero's $$ Seafood

1583 Coal Harbour Quay. 604-669-7666. www.carderos.com.

Perched on a pier on Coal Harbour, between downtown and Stanley Park, Cardero's offers almost every dining party a luminescent view of the yachts moored at the nearby marina. The menu hews to seafood mainstays—you can't go wrong with the fish and chips, the grilled salmon is done just right, and the shrimp-topped Caesar salad does justice to both salads and seafood. Call ahead for a window table to get the best view.

CinCin Ristorante

$$ Mediterranean

1154 Robson St. 604-688-7338. www.cincin.net.

Mustard-colored stucco walls, brick trim and wood-fired ovens combine to give this bustling bistro a warm, Mediterranean air. The stylish Italian cuisine melds traditional dishes with gourmet embellishments—fire-roasted chicken pastas and risottos, pizzas cooked in the wood-fired oven, and shellfish pots.

Montri's Thai

$$ Thai

3629 W. Broadway. 604-738-9888. www.montri-thai.com.

Vancouver diners perennially vote this the city's best Thai restaurant. It's famed for its tom yum goong (sour seafood soup) and massaman curries, hearty, thick concoctions with beef and potatoes. Swimming angels—chicken with spinach stir-fry—is another favourite. The cozy, family atmosphere reflects its West Kitsilano neighbourhood.

Pink Pearl

$$ Chinese

1132 E. Hastings St. 604-253-4316. www.pinkpearl.com.

Every morning at the crack of dawn, the dim sum cooks arrive at Pink Pearl to start preparing the day's delicacies. Every day near noon, cars and taxis start to pull up, disgorging workers from downtown who come for a dim sum lunch. By 12:30pm the vast room is packed, and the dim sum ladies are plying the aisles with baskets and plates of dumplings, rolls, cakes and stuffed pastries—vegetarian, seafood, fruit- or meat-filled; rice, wheat or taro flour; hot, sweet, sour or all three. By 2pm, the day's selection is depleted, so don't come late.

Sawasdee

$$ Thai

4250 Main St. 604-876-4030.

Vancouver's first Thai restaurant still excels at blending BC ingredients with Thai dishes. Duck curry is a standout; so is the green curry (with chicken or shrimp). Many consider Swasdee's pad Thai the city's best. The softly lit stucco interior lends a tropical air, and the menu offers that most wonderful of Thai desserts, black-rice pudding.

Shabusen Yakiniku House

$$ Japanese/Korean/Sushi

2993 Granville St. (at 14th Ave). 604-737-6888.

This place is hopping at lunchtime, so arrive early or make reservations. You can order from the menu, but most in the know choose the buffet, and use the

BBQ grill in the middle of the tables to cook their own selection. For lighter fare—or as appetizers for a full meal—the sushi selection is among the best in town.

Vij's $$ Indian

480 W. 11th Ave. Dinner only. 604-736-6664. www.vijs.ca.

Diners literally make pilgrimages here from across Canada to experience Vikram Vij's edgy Indian cuisine. The no-reservations policy means dinner hopefuls line up early and wait patiently. What's the draw? The astounding culinary inventions, such as buttermilk curry, ghee-braised short ribs in a red-wine-cinnamon curry, or lamb "popsicles" in cream curry.

Bojangles $ American

785 Denman St. 604-987-7555. www.bojanglescafe.com.

Perched on a sunny corner in the West End, Bojangles is the perfect place to stop before or after a trek around the Stanley Park seawall. Sandwiches, soups and salads, and pastries are the fare here—nothing memorable, but well-made, and economical. The turkey-cranberry sandwich is tasty, and the soup of the day is invariably thick and filling. Grab one of the south-facing outdoor tables on a sunny day.

Buddhist Vegetarian Restaurant $ Chinese

137 E. Pender St. 604-683-8816.

With a decent dim sum menu, and a reliable inventory of meat-free dishes (mostly bowls of noodles and vegetables), Buddhist Vegetarian makes up in value and taste what it lacks in ambience. Like so many Chinatown eateries, the décor leans toward formica—but the signature dish, Eight Treasures Soup, is a tureen so flavourful and filling it can feed two for the price of one dinner at most restaurants.

Crêpe la Bretonne $ French

795 Jervis St. 604-608-1266.

Crêpes are simple in concept—egg-and-flour batter, lightly sautéed, folded and filled. It's the execution that demands skill. This West End cafe's owner is from Brittany, and the crêpes here are traditional (you can get buckwheat flour) and very, very light. If you want dinner, have your crêpes filled with ham and cheese; dessert, apples; breakfast, ham and well, cheese again. It's nothing fancy, but crêpes make a quick, tasty meal. A selection of French hard ciders rounds out the menu.

Stepho's $ Greek

1124 Davie St. 604-683-2555.

Sometimes the line to get into Stepho's stretches out the door, down the street and around the corner. All those people come for heaping platters of Greek roast lamb, potatoes, salad and vegetables—an utterly filling, economical meal that will last all day. Yes, they have baklava, but it's hard to find the room after finishing off a dinner platter.

Vera's Burger Shack $ Burgers

1181 Denman St. 604-681-5450; www.verasburgershack.com (multiple locations).

Vancouver burger-lovers know they can count on one of the several Vera's locations for their fix—and hungry kids craving something quick and "normal" will leave satisfied without breaking the bank.

Dining on Vancouver Island

Sooke Harbour House $$$$ West Coast

Whiffen Spit Rd., Sooke. Follow Hwy. 14 West from Victoria. 250-642-3421 or 800-889-9688. www.sookeharbourhouse.com. 28 rooms.

When Sinclair and Frederique Philip opened a small inn in the mid-1970s to offer New Wave cuisine based on exotic, local ingredients, virtually no one in Canada was exploring those culinary frontiers. Today an entire cuisine (West Coast) borrows their pioneering principles, and Sooke Harbour House is quite simply the most famous restaurant in Canada. Gourmands fly across the continent to have dinner here—what they find every night is different, but always draws on local seafood (oysters, sea cucumbers, rockfish, seaweed) and fresh vegetables, herbs and fruits grown in the inn's extensive gardens.

Bengal Lounge $$$ Indian

721 Government St., in the Empress Hotel, Victoria. 250-389-2727. www.fairmont.com.

The Empress Hotel's less-formal dining room is redolent with Empire atmosphere—polished mahogany, ceiling fans, potted palms, red-leather armchairs, even a tiger skin on the wall. The lounge actually dates back to the 1950s and is noted for its inventive array of martinis and tropical drinks, and its splendid selection of curries. At lunch, a long table is laden with ingredients for the curry buffet, ranging from coconut-chicken to mango chutney. Dinner à la carte offerings include curry flambé. Now that's imperial.

Café Brio $$$ Northern Italian

944 Fort St., Victoria. Dinner only. 250-383-0009. www.cafe-brio.com.

A decade after pioneering bistro cuisine in Victoria, Café Brio finds its popularity unabated. The intriguing décor (Modigliani-style nudes on the walls, unadorned fir-plank floors, 18ft ceilings) combines with excellent Northern Italian cooking. Braised breast of veal, and scallops on rosemary polenta, are typical dishes. Some of the more sought after booths are reserved weeks ahead in peak season.

Paprika $$$ French

2524 Estevan Ave., Victoria. Dinner only. 250-592-7424. www.paprika-bistro.com.

Neighbourhood bistros have risen like Victoria's spring flowers in the capital city over the past decade, and Paprika is the best of the bunch. The French provincial cuisine relies on fresh island ingredients—farm-grown duck, lamb and pork; fresh-picked wild mushrooms; seafood from the Strait of Georgia. A sumptuous bisque, either shellfish or lobster, starts the meal every evening. Simply roasted or braised meats and fish mark the entrée selections.

Ming's $$ Chinese

1321 Quadra St., Victoria. 250-385-4405. www.mings.ca.

Though it occasionally ventures into Szechuan or Hunan cuisine, Ming's is classic Mandarin in Victoria's Chinatown. After you enter the dining room through an ivory moongate, service is infinitely attentive, and all the usuals are on the menu, from sweet-and-sour pork to fried rice. The most interesting dishes include sweet-and-sour duck, ginger beef, and a scrumptious Buddhist delicacy, vegetarian *lo han jai.*

Spinnaker's Brewpub $$ Canadian Regional

308 Catherine St., Victoria. 250-386-2739. www.spinnakers.com.

Spinnaker's claims to be the first licensed brewpub in Canada—a distinction it enhances considerably with this nifty restaurant perched beside the Inner Harbour. The heritage Craftsman building holds the brewpub, restaurant, outdoor deck, and a sundries shop in which you can buy such marvels as malt vinegar made from their ale. Dining fare is upscale pub food, such as a tasting plate of island artisan cheeses, a braised-lamb sandwich, and yeast-battered fish and chips. The brews are highly flavoured, and very, very fresh.

Blue Fox $ North American

919 Fort St., Victoria. 250-380-1683.

It's easy to find the Blue Fox: just look for the line out on the sidewalk, especially for weekend breakfasts or weekday lunches. The fare here is not exotic—breakfast platters piled high with hotcakes, thick toast, fat omelettes and sausages. Lunch and dinner bring out big handmade hamburgers and hand-cut fries and meatloaf. Breakfast is served all day, if your patience is tested by the morning lines.

Common Loaf Bake Shop $ Bakery

80 First St., Tofino. 250-725-3915.

The loaves at this counterculture hangout in Tofino are far from common—the thick and nutty multi-grain concoctions are a meal in themselves. There's also excellent coffee, a luscious lineup of pastries, muffins and scones in the morning, and simple soups and salads for lunch and dinner. The cedar-and-fir panelled ambience is pure New Age, and the bulletin board is the place to find out what's happening in the West Coast alternative community, from Reiki classes to logging protests.

The properties listed below were selected for their ambience, location and/or value for money. Prices reflect the average cost for a standard double room for two people (not including applicable city or provincial taxes). Hotels in Vancouver constantly offer special discount packages. Price ranges quoted do not reflect the city hotel tax of 10%. Properties are located in Vancouver, unless otherwise specified.

$$$$$ over $350 $$ $100–$175
$$$$ $250–$350 $ less than $100
$$$ $175–$250

Luxury

Fairmont Waterfront $$$$$ 489 rooms

900 Canada Place. 604-691-1991 or 800-441-1414. www.fairmont.com/waterfront.
The Waterfront is the Fairmont chain's downtown business hotel, a gleaming steel-and-glass tower in which every room has an expansive view—60 percent of the rooms overlook Burrard Inlet, Stanley Park and the North Shore. The rooms are furnished in crisp cream tones, maple and oak and marble. An extensive health club, business centre, shopping arcade and **Herons Restaurant ($$$)** round out the facilities. Canada Place sits across the street.

Four Seasons $$$$$ 376 rooms

791 W. Georgia St. 604-689-9333 or 800-819-3053. www.fourseasons.com/vancouver.
Attentive service is the hallmark at one of Vancouver's consistently top-rated hotels—if a doorman sees you returning from a jog, he'll hand you a towel and water bottle. Though not overly large, the guest rooms are elegantly furnished, with brass trim, wood tones and marble baths. Hotel facilities are lavish, including an indoor-outdoor pool that opens out onto a huge second-storey garden terrace.

Opus Hotel

$$$$$ 97 rooms

322 Davie St. 604 642-6787. www.opushotel.com.

Designers of this utterly distinctive hotel in Yale-town chose unusual décor elements to echo the property's hip neighbourhood. Candles and settees are the lobby furnishings; headset-adorned staffers greet guests at reception podiums. Rooms feature strong colours such as purple and ebony, and bathrooms have floor-to-ceiling windows, and a counter made from a long stone slab.

Pan Pacific

$$$$$ 504 rooms

999 Canada Place. 604-662-8111 or 800-937-1515 (US), 800-663-1515 (Canada). www.vancouver.panpacific.com.

Perched on the shoreward end of the Canada Place pier, the Pan Pacific's white-sided tower faces water on three sides, so virtually all the rooms have expansive views of Burrard Inlet. Asian flair flavours the famously attentive service, which relies on a small army of staffers to meet guest needs. The rooms are compact but luxuriously outfitted, with teak and marble touches.

Fairmont Hotel Vancouver

$$$$ 556 rooms

900 W. Georgia St. 604-684-3131 or 800-441-1414. www.fairmont.com/hotelvancouver.

The Hotel Van is a Canadian icon, one of the string of chateau-style landmark hotels spread across the country by its railroads. Steep gables and copper roofs characterize the familiar Vancouver landmark. Rooms often contain unaltered historic elements such as tiled baths with deep soaking tubs. Every service imaginable is on-site, including a lavish health club with a glass-roofed pool. **Griffins ($$)** is undisputedly the best place for breakfast in downtown.

Sutton Place Hotel $$$$ 397 rooms

845 Burrard St. 604-682-5511 or 866-378-8866. www.vancouver.suttonplace.com.

 There's hardly a minute that no limousine is waiting in the driveway of the pink palace on Burrard that remains the film industry's favourite place to stay in Vancouver. Snazzy guest rooms have huge picture windows, magenta and beige décor and marble baths. The service is expert and unquestioning, and every amenity imaginable is offered, from an extensive fitness facility to (naturally) 24-hour room service.

Wedgewood Hotel $$$$ 83 rooms

845 Hornby St. 604-689-7777 or 800-663-0666. www.wedgewoodhotel.com.

 Loyal fans of this discreet boutique hotel consider it one of Vancouver's best. Owner Eleni Skalbania chose the distinctive French and Italian décor for the spacious suites, outfitted with brocade-covered couches, in-room host bars and balconies overlooking the Law Courts. The service is attentive, and a new spa adds to the compact health club; **Bacchus** restaurant *(see Must Eat)* and lounge are on the ground floor. The Vancouver Art Gallery and Robson Street shopping are just minutes away.

Moderate

Granville Island Hotel $$$ 85 rooms

1253 Johnston St. 604-683-7373 or 800-663-1840. www.granvilleislandhotel.com.

The metal-panel siding of this two-storey property reflects the industrial heritage of Granville Island—but the interior is utterly contemporary, with spacious rooms furnished in post-Modern metal and glass, and red and blue fabrics. The hotel faces False Creek, and sits at the quiet end of its namesake island, where cafes, stalls and galleries are just minutes away. Amenities include a full health club, restaurant and bar. Pets are welcome for a modest fee.

Hotel LeSoleil $$$ 119 rooms

567 Hornby St. 604-632-3000 or 877-632-3030. www.lesoleilhotel.com.

The two massive Expressionist canvases in the lobby set the tone at this lush downtown boutique hotel—tropical scenes with languorous figures hint at indulgence. The rooms continue this theme, with down-pillowed beds, brocade fabrics in burgundy and forest green and hushed lighting. Le Soleil caused a stir in 2002 by offering rooms for a half-day, midday, and it made no bones about what they were for. Its downtown location is close to Canada Place, Stanley Park, the Art Gallery and Gastown.

St. Regis

$$$ 72 rooms

602 Dunsmuir St. 604-681-1135 or 800-770-7929. www.stregishotel.com.

There's nothing fancy about the St. Regis, whose rooms are compact, furnished in muted beige tones, quiet and air-conditioned. The mid-downtown location is close to Canada Place, Gastown and Chinatown. The hotel offers a business centre, Internet access, and a fitness facility, but no on-site parking.

Listel Vancouver

$$$ 130 rooms

1300 Robson St. 604-684-8461 or 800-663-5491. www.listel-vancouver.com.

Local art is the distinguishing element at this snazzy boutique hotel on Robson. Rooms on gallery floors are decorated with works from the hotel's alliance with a nearby upscale art dealer; one floor features First Nations art derived from an affiliation with the UBC Museum of Anthropology. Spacious suites have Berber carpet, beige and maroon hues, and cozy window seats. The location is ideal for visiting Stanley Park and the Vancouver Art Gallery, and for watching the bustling scene on Robson.

Residences on Georgia

$$$ 493 rooms

1288 W. Georgia St. 604-891-6101. www.respal.com.

These snazzy modern apartments are an ideal choice for longer-stay visitors to Vancouver. Furnished in muted gray, white, beige and brushed-metal trim, with small kitchenettes, breakfast nooks and small office spaces, they appeal to film-industry workers in town for shoots. There's a screening room downstairs, as well as access to a huge health club across the street, gated underground parking and private-access security. Weekly and monthly rates compare favourably to moderate hotel accommodations.

Thistledown House

$$$ 7 rooms

3910 Capilano Rd., North Vancouver. 604-986-7173 or 888-633-7173. www.thistle-down.com.

Venerable apple trees shade the backyard patio of this restored timber tycoon's North Shore mansion. The genteel Arts and Crafts-style house features stunning built-in cabinetry, especially in the formal dining room where guests enjoy sumptuous breakfasts—house-made pastries and preserves, omelettes and French toast. Guest rooms have Victorian furnishings such as walnut four-poster beds, and the luxurious honeymoon suite boasts a heated bathroom floor and a sitting room with fireplace.

Budget

North Vancouver Hotel $$ 71 rooms

1800 Capilano Rd., North Vancouver. 604-987-4461 or 800-663-4055.
www.northvancouverhotel.ca.

This colourful stucco facility is a top-notch motel with an excellent location.
Spacious rooms, decorated in pastel fabrics, are located in quiet buildings
set back from the road. A palm-bordered swimming pool, free local calls and
continental breakfast round out the amenities. The setting is ideal for visiting
Grouse Mountain, Capilano Bridge and park, and lies within a half-hour of the
Horseshoe Bay ferry terminal.

Sylvia Hotel $$ 119 rooms

1154 Gilford St. 604-681-9321. www.sylviahotel.com.

Many is the family whose Sylvia loyalty spans generations—it is by far the best
economical hotel in downtown Vancouver, and it's the one closest to Stanley
Park to boot (with parking included). The rooms and suites are like mid-20C
apartments, with polyglot furnishings, little discernible décor scheme, ample
closets and sitting rooms. Many have kitchenettes—real ones, with refrigerators, stoves, sinks and counter space. The ivy-covered brick building is a World
War I-era landmark facing English Bay and the southeast end of the seawall
pedestrian path

Hostelling International $ 282 rooms

1025 Granville St. (Central); 604-685-5335 or 888-203-8333; 226 rooms. 1114 Burnaby
St. (Downtown); 604-684-4565 or 888-203-4302; 223 rooms. 1515 Discovery St. (Jericho
Beach); 604-224-3208 or 888-203-4303. www.hihostels.ca.

All three of Vancouver's hostels offer excellent locations.
Rooms (both dorm-style and private) are clean and up-
dated. Full facilities range from media rooms to laundries
and cafes, as well as on-staff information services. The
downtown location is on a quiet street near Stanley Park;
the central location is handy to Granville Island, Gastown
and the city's entertainment district. The Jericho Beach
hostel is closest to Kitsilano and the University of British
Columbia, and offers free shuttle service downtown.

Shaughnessy Village $ 240 rooms

1125 W. 12th Ave. 604-736-5512. www.shaughnessyvillage.com.

At 13 storeys, this edifice southeast of downtown advertises itself as the
world's largest B&B. That's a claim hard to dispute, but more significant is the
fact it offers comfy housing at highly affordable rates. The 240 rooms are
compact—resembling ship's berths, with wood trim and maroon tones—but
well-outfitted nonetheless, with private baths. Virtually all the facilities of a
major hotel are on-site, including a swimming pool and a restaurant where an
English/continental breakfast is served, as well as a billiards room, an Internet
cafe, a spa and a tanning facility. What more could you want?

YWCA Hotel/Residence $ 115 rooms

733 Beatly St. 604-895-5830 or 800-663-1424. www.ywcahotel.com.

A wide variety of rooms is available in this new facility in the east end of downtown, from dorm-style to small kitchenette family suites. A laundry, coffee shop, parking and in-room refrigerators round out the facilities; weekly and monthly rates are available. The location is close to Chinatown and the city's stadium district. Of course, the exercise facilities here are extensive.

Staying in Vancouver Island and Whistler

The Fairmont Château Whistler $$$$$ 550 rooms

4599 Chateau Blvd., Whistler. 604-938-8000. 800-441-1414. www.fairmont.com/whistler.

Though this is one of the most upscale accommodations in Whistler, the ambience is not all palatial. The building itself, at the foot of Blackcomb Mountain, is indeed chateau-like, and the lobby, common areas and Wildflower restaurant are all refined and elegant. But the 500 rooms, outfitted in country wood furniture, are relaxed and spacious—and virtually all have a view of snowcapped peaks. The proximity of the lifts means the Château is a ski-in, ski-out property.

Wickaninnish Inn $$$$$ 76 rooms

Chesterman Beach, 2mi south of Tofino. 250-725-3100 or 800-333-4604. www.wickinn.com.

When Tofino native Charles McDiarmid opened this lodge in the early 1990s, he had a radical idea: the West Coast shore could be as appealing a destination in winter as in summer. So he designed the stone-and-timber main building with huge, sturdy plate-glass windows facing the ocean, and positioned the rooms so the winter tempests could be seen while visitors enjoyed the comforts of firelight and cozy beds. Most rooms at the Wick feature balconies facing the water, many have soaking

tubs. The Wick's spa (see Must Be Pampered) is a destination in itself, and the Pointe Restaurant ($$$$) is famed for its innovative cuisine.

The Fairmont Empress $$$$ 477 rooms

721 Government St., Victoria. 250-384-8111 or 800-441-1414. www.fairmont.com/empress.

Rooms in this landmark are as elegant as the building they occupy, with late Victorian furnishings of walnut and brocade, spacious dimensions and every modern amenity. Every Victoria visitor should stay at the Empress at least once. It's best to be on a higher floor, as the street out front, Government, is the city's main thoroughfare. There's a premium on rooms facing the Inner Harbour, so you might get a better room at a more reasonable rate on the back side of the hotel. All that said, cost should be a secondary consideration—this is one of the great hotels of the world.

Haterleigh Heritage Inn

$$$$ 6 rooms

243 Kingston St., Victoria. 250-384-9995. www.haterleigh.com.

The stained-glass windows in this lavish 1901 house let light pour into the crystal-and-brass decorated lobby. Most of the guest rooms have whirlpool tubs, and are furnished with Victorian antiques. Breakfasts are hearty British-style affairs, with eggs, scones, pastries and sausage. Guests enjoy complimentary afternoon tea and evening sherry.

Magnolia Hotel & Spa

$$$$ 63 rooms

623 Courtney St., Victoria. 250-381-0999 or 877-624-6654. www.magnoliahotel.com.

Opulence rules at this Victorian-style boutique hotel. Mahogany walls, alabaster chandeliers and a gold gilt ceiling greet visitors in the compact lobby. All the rooms and suites are spacious, with floor-to-ceiling windows that let in ample light to complement the cream-and-beige décor. Large bathrooms have separate walk-in showers and soaking tubs. A long list of amenities ranges from a wet bar and fridge in every room to a full-service Aveda day spa in the hotel. The location is ideal for walking to Fort Street, Old Town, Chinatown and the Inner Harbour.

Bedford Regency

$$$ 40 rooms

1140 Government St., Victoria. 250-384-6835 or 800-665-6500. www.bedfordregency.com.

Located a short walk away from the Inner Harbour and Government Street shops, this boutique hotel has handsomely appointed guest rooms with wood-burning fireplaces, large cushy chairs and goose-down duvets. Some rooms feature whirlpool tubs, flower-bedecked window boxes and views of James Bay. Pub fare is served on the premises in the English-style **Garrick's Head ($$)**.

Fairholme Manor

$$$ 4 suites

4638 Rockland Place, Victoria. 250-598-3240 or 877-511-3322. www.fairholmemanor.com.

This elegant mansion occupies a serene, large lot atop Rockland Hill, next to Government House. The 1885 Italianate mansion is 7,000sq ft; the two suites in the main house boast high ceilings, bay windows overlooking the garden, and expansive baths with deep tubs. Breakfast is European, but not continental—multiple courses include eggs and pastries.

Long Beach Lodge
$$$ 41 rooms, 10 cottages

1441 Pacific Rim Hwy., Tofino. 250-725-2442 or 877-844-7873.
www.longbeachlodgeresort.com.

Warm, comfortable tones of wood domi-
nate both the décor and the atmosphere
at this beachfront lodge in Tofino. The
lobby and public spaces feature huge
Douglas-fir beams and trim; the exterior is
cedar shake, with metal roofing and stone
accents. A cheery fire crackles in the large
stone fireplace indoors. Rooms are done
in handmade fir furniture, with sizable
soaking tubs and balconies or patios overlooking the ocean; amenities include
small refrigerators and coffee makers. It's steps away from a 1.6km/mile-long
broad sand beach, with enticing headlands at either end. Pacific Rim National
Park is just a few kilometres south of the lodge.

Rosewood Victoria Inn
$$$ 17 rooms

595 Michigan St., Victoria. 250-384-6641 or 866-986-2222. www.rosewoodvictoria.com.

The sunny yellow exterior of this small inn near the Parliament Buildings hints
at the cozy warmth inside. The airy courtyard lets in light, and the cheery
wallpaper and floral fabrics in the rooms continue the country theme. Each in-
dividually decorated room has a balcony or patio. Rates include a three-course
breakfast served in the conservatory or on the heated patio.

Summit Lodge
$$$ 81 rooms

4359 Main St, Whistler. 804-932-2778 or 888-913-8811. www.summitlodge.com.

The Kimpton Hotel group specializes in low-
key but expertly run boutique hotels, and
their Whistler property is a sterling example.
The comfortable rooms here have compact
kitchenettes, country pine furniture and
balconies; the service is friendly and knowl-
edgeable; and the location in the middle of
Whistler Village is handy to on-mountain
activities and village life. There's also a pool
and a small fitness centre and spa. Not only is breakfast included in the room
rate, they'll bring it to your room at a designated time.

Whistler Hostel International
$ 7 rooms

5678 Alta Lake Rd., Whistler. 604-932-5492. www.hihostels.ca.

Located within a 10-minute drive from Whistler Village, this hostel hugs the
shore of Alta Lake, and offers 32 beds in shared or private quarters to members
and nonmembers alike. Amenities include a guest kitchen, a living room with
a fireplace, a sauna and bicycle storage. Bikes can be rented and there's free
canoe rental.

Index

Index

Photo Credits:

Aerie Resort 100; BC Place Stadium 41; Boat Cruises Vancouver 60; C Restaurant 110; Capilano Suspension Bridge 83; Chris Cameron, Coastal Jazz 9; Christ Church Cathedral, Martin Knowles 42; CinCin Ristorante 112; Cioppino's Mediterranean Grill 110; City of Vancouver Archives 20; Diva 110; Fairholme Manor 122; The Fairmont Château Whistler 103, 121; Fairmont Empress 91, 114, 121; Fairmont Hotel Vancouver 43, 78, 116-117; ©Eric J. Fletcher 44; Granville Island Ferries, Inc. 56; Granville Island Model Trains Museum 9, 53; ©Grouse Mountain Resort 80-87 (icon); Gulf of Georgia Cannery NHS, Anders Galasso 5; Harrison Hot Springs Resort & Spa 86; Haterleigh Heritage Inn 122; ©Al Harvey 4, 7, 40, 44, 45, 46, 56, 72, 73, 74, 84; Hell's Gate Airtram, D. McKinney 86; Hostelling International 120; Kimpton Group Hotels 123; Listel Vancouver 119; Long Beach Lodge 123; Lumiere 108; Eric P. Lucas 28, 64, 65, 104, 105, 106; H.R. MacMillan Space Centre 66; Maplewood Farm, Bill Staley 67.

MICHELIN: 58, 92; Gwen Cannon 7, 26, 33, 47, 50, 82, 85, 89, 92, 94; ©Brigitta L. House 36, 75; John Thompson 93.

Ming's 115; Mission Hill Family Estate 5, 107; Opus Hotel 117; Pan Pacific 117; Parcs Canada, W. McIntyre 97; PhotoDisc© 34, 111, 112, 115; Pink Pearl 112; Roedde House Museum 55; Royal BC Museum Corp. 90; ©Tom Ryan 8, 30, 87; Science World British Columbia 67; Sooke Harbour House 114; St. Regis 119; Sutton Place Hotel 78, 108-109, 110, 118; ©Tim Thompson/Apa Publications 3, 18-19, 38, 58; Tourism Vancouver Island 61, 62, 63, 98, 99, 101; Tourism Victoria ©Photosure.com 5, 9, 93, 95, 96; UBC Botanical Garden 29; UBC Museum of Anthropology, Bill McLennan 6, 48, 49.

Tourism Vancouver: ©Al Harvey 4, 24, 25, 80; ©Tom Ryan 4, 6, 7, 21, 22, 23, 24, 27, 31, 32, 35, 40-47 (icon), 54, 57, 81.

Vancouver Civic Theatres 8, 68, 69, 70; Vancouver Maritime Museum 51; Vancouver Museum 52; Vancouver Public Library 41; VBIA 37; Vida Wellness Spa 79; Wedgewood Hotel 76, 118; Whistler Resort Assn., Paul Morrison 8, 102; Wickaninnish Inn 121; Yale Hotel 77.

Cover photos:
Front Cover: ©Tim Thompson/Apa Publications; Front Cover small left: Image courtesy of Cypress Mountain, www.cypressmountain.com; Front Cover small right: ©Tom Ryan. Back Cover: ©Mark Malleson, www.killerwhalephotography.com.

YOUR OPINION MATTERS!

Thank you for purchasing a Michelin Travel Publications product. To help us continue to offer you the absolute best in travel guides, maps and atlases, we need your feedback.

Please fill in this questionnaire and return it to:
Michelin Apa Publications, Ltd.
Attn: Marketing
3636 33rd Street
Long Island City, NY 11106

To thank you, we will draw one name from the returned questionnaires each month. Each month's winner will receive a free Michelin 2008 North American Road Atlas.

1. How would you rate the following features of the product, if applicable?
   1 = *Very Good*   **2** = *Acceptable*   **3** = *Poor*

	1	2	3
Selection of attractions/sights	❏	❏	❏
Practical Information (prices, etc.)	❏	❏	❏
Description of establishments	❏	❏	❏
General presentation	❏	❏	❏
Cover	❏	❏	❏

2. How satisfied were you with this product?

❏ Very satisfied ❏ Satisfied ❏ Somewhat Satisfied ❏ Not Satisfied

If not satisfied, how should we improve the product? _____

_____

3. Did you buy this product: *(check all that apply)*
   ❏ For holiday/vacation
   ❏ For short breaks or weekends
   ❏ For business purposes
   ❏ As a gift
   ❏ Other

4. Where would you buy and expect our products to be available?
   (check all that apply)

   ❏ Supermarket   ❏ Mass Merchandiser
   ❏ Convenience store ❏ Specialty store (museum shop, travel store, etc.)
   ❏ Bookstore   ❏ Gas/Service Station
   ❏ Online   ❏ Kiosk/Gift shop

5. Which destinations do you visit the most often for pleasure? *(list as many locations as you wish)* _____

_____

Tear Here

6. Which destinations do you visit the most often for business? *(list as many locations as you wish)* _____

_____

7. When you go on vacation, generally how long do you stay? *(check all that apply)*
- ❏ Three or four days
- ❏ One week
- ❏ Two weeks
- ❏ Short (three or four days) and one week vacations
- ❏ Other _____

8. When you travel, what mode of transportation do you most frequently use? *(1 – most frequent, 6 – least frequent)*

____Plane ____Car ____Bus ____Train ____Cruise ____Other

9. Would you consider buying other Michelin travel books or products?
- ❏ Yes ❏ No

If yes, which one(s):
- ❏ Must SEES
- ❏ North American Maps
- ❏ European Maps
- ❏ North American Travel Guides
- ❏ European Travel Guides
- ❏ Hotel and Restaurants Guides

10. Your age?
- ❏ Less than 25 years old ❏ 25–35 years old ❏ 36–45 years old
- ❏ 46–55 years old ❏ 56–65 years old ❏ 65 years plus

11. Additional Comments:

_____

_____

Telephone or e-mail where we may reach you: _____

If you would like to be added to our mailing list, please fill out the information below:

❏ Ms. ❏ Mrs. ❏ Mr.

Name _____

Address _____

City_____ State _____

Zip Code_____ Country_____

If you would like to be added to our e-mail list for special offers and updates, please provide your e-mail adress. All e-mail addresses are kept confidential and are not shared with outside companies.

_____